UNDER FIRE

UNDER FIRE

13 RULES FOR SURVIVING
CANCEL CULTURE
(AND OTHER CRISES)

WESLEY DONEHUE

LIONCREST
PUBLISHING

UNDER FIRE

13 Rules for Surviving Cancel Culture and Other Crises

ISBN   978-1-5445-2725-3   *Hardcover*
         978-1-5445-2723-9   *Paperback*
         978-1-5445-2724-6   *Ebook*
         978-1-5445-2726-0   *Audiobook*

This book is dedicated to PETA,

*because the only thing better than the taste
of bacon is the joy of kicking your ass.*

CONTENTS

INTRODUCTION

When people ask me about what I do, I sometimes refer them to one of my favorite movies, *Pulp Fiction*—particularly the character named Winston Wolf, played by Harvey Keitel. In the movie, a crisis occurs when the lead characters accidentally shoot a guy in their car in a blood-filled scene. They go to hide at a friend's house, and the guys start freaking out until their boss tells them to calm down: "I've called the Wolf."

Soon there is a knock at the door, and the visitor says, "I'm Winston Wolf. I solve problems."

He is the fixer, the cleaner. Being a Winston Wolf means being a person who solves problems—usually with brilliant, lucid thinking under pressure.

Well, when it comes to the crisis du jour, I'm your Winston Wolf. Crisis is in my DNA.

For many—maybe even most—people, turbulent times are periodic and sporadic, the painful exceptions in their lives, with plenty of breathing room between flare-ups. But for me, crisis has always been the rule. These days, I make crises my business (literally), helping leaders in politics and business navigate treacherous waters when, in a moment, their worlds are turned upside down.

My ability to handle tough situations and drama was born out of what I faced and endured as a child. I grew in a perpetual storm. It was routine for me to be in the fire. In fact, it was *not* being in the fire that was uncomfortable for me. I thought all families were filled with daily drama. I thought all families yelled at each other all the time. I thought it was normal for family members to beat other family members into a bloody pulp.

I didn't know any different.

Because I was born into chaos, I learned early on how to keep my cool while everyone else was freaking out as their worlds fell apart. That's how and why I'm able to step into a crisis-laden situation and put together a plan of counteraction. My skills were forged in the fires of chronic family meltdown.

Obviously, my childhood was tough. We were dirt poor, and my father was very abusive. My sister and I watched him beat our mother right in front of us. I remember one time when he was so violent that we hid under my bed while he knocked Mom's teeth out. Another time, he threw Mom into the trunk of our car, put us in the back seat, and then drove us down a dirt road. When we stopped, he dragged Mom out of the trunk by her hair and put the barrel of his shotgun in her mouth.

"Say goodbye to your Mom!" he shouted at us.

When they finally split up, dad put a pistol in his mouth and said, "You're going to tell the judge you want to live with me, or I'm going to blow my brains out!"

I was eight years old when that happened.

After my parents' divorce, we were nearly homeless. Frankly, if it wasn't for government programs, we wouldn't have had a roof over our heads. Dad was a deadbeat—he never paid a dime of support. He eventually remarried, but he beat his new wife, too, and she left. He was eventually arrested for dealing drugs. There were stints in prison.

So Mom was pretty much a single mother, raising us in Section-8 housing. I was one of the only white kids in the neighborhood. We lived off food stamps and other government handouts. I remember being so poor that my sister and I had to find and pick up pennies on the road so Mom could put gas in the car.

She went to cosmetology school so she could earn a paycheck. She also remarried. We eventually moved from being dirt poor to being lower-middle class during those formative years in my life.

My only real escape from the storms that seemed to always swirl around me was reading comic books and watching reruns of *Star Trek* and the three *Star Wars* movies over and over again. I was a huge nerd long before it became cool.

When I was in my early teens, my mom developed a degenerative back disease. The doctor speculated that it came from all of the beatings she had experienced. She was in a lot of pain. So the doctor prescribed opioids. She was on them throughout my high school years, and by the time I got to college, she had been in and out of rehab several times.

Today, both of my parents are gone. Mom died of an opioid overdose in 2004, three weeks before a US Senate race that I was working on. A few years later, my dad was battling cancer and near death. I thought he was dying because of the disease, but when he was on his deathbed, his doctor told me that what was really killing him was his addiction to meth. His immune system was virtually wiped out by the drugs. It was sad. He looked like the poster child for meth addiction—nothing more than just skin and bones, teeth and hair falling out, patches all over his skin, and scabs on his face. He seemed less than human.

PEACE IN A STORM

All of these experiences created in me the ability to deal with tough situations. I noticed that when a crisis struck and everyone around me was freaking out, I was able to keep my cool. It was almost like I could find peace in the middle of a storm. This ability enables me to react strategically and quickly when confronting a crisis.

I also learned a thing or two about street fighting for survival. I was a bit of a brawler as a kid. Growing up in an environment of violence, I learned to do what I had to do.

When I was a teenager in Goose Creek, South Carolina, we moved to a new school district. I didn't want to go to the new school because there had been a drive-by shooting in the school parking lot. I wound up going to a school board meeting and speaking to them.

While there, I met a state senator named Bill Mescher who was paying attention to the issue and appreciated the stand I was taking. Senator Mescher asked me if I wanted to work on his campaign. I did, and it was a great learning experience for me. When I got to college, Mescher asked me if I wanted to become a senate page for him.

While working as a page, I went to the University of South Carolina, where I majored in engineering because I wanted to be Scotty from *Star Trek*. I soon found that my early experiences in politics had awakened something in me, and I eventually switched my major to political science. I even ran for student body president, but I got booted from the race for fighting with one of my opponents. I lost it, really, throwing him on a table and kicking him. It was like my street-fighting from childhood had found its way back to the surface. Still, I managed to become the state chair of College Republicans, and I worked on every single campaign I could find.

That's how I met Rod Shealy.

ORIGINS OF A POLITICAL HITMAN

Rod was a political consultant who had worked on numerous local and statewide campaigns. He was a mad genius. Early on, he had worked with Lee Atwater, who served as an advisor to Ronald Reagan and George H. W. Bush. Shealy gave me my first paying campaign job.

At the time, I didn't know such jobs existed; I had been a volunteer up to this point. No guidance counselor in school had ever mentioned anything about being a lobbyist or political consultant. But Rod Shealy, an eccentric guy with a big bushy beard who liked to wear Hawaiian shirts with his chest hair sticking out, known for chewing a cigar all day, opened the door to a whole new world for me. For the first time, I understood that politics could be an actual job.

So I made the jump from volunteer to recruit. Soon, I was working with state senators and even the lieutenant governor of South Carolina. I also did a lot of grassroots work, which is where I learned how to count votes and all about presents, micro targeting, and weight. With Rod Shealy, it was all about the numbers, and I learned from the best.

Eventually, I met a guy named Terry Sullivan, and he soon became my mentor. He invited me to work with him on Jim DeMint's campaign for the Senate in 2003. It was really a longshot race. DeMint was a little-known congressman running against some very heavy hitters in South Carolina. But we worked hard to get him elected. After that, Terry asked me to help create and run his company, First Tuesday Strategies, where I worked for five years.

Then I started Push Digital, one of the first Republican digital agencies, a company dedicated to fighting for candidates, causes, and corporations that strengthen America's economy to provide better lives for everyday Americans.

CANCEL CULTURE RUN AMOK

When I was growing up (yes, back in my day), the main news stations were ABC, NBC, and CBS, each of which had a one-hour show every night that presented a distilled, factual news hour. Now, however, we have a twenty-four-hour news network, and that means that twenty-four hours' worth of news has to be filled on multiple stations all day every day. Events that never would have been mentioned before now become stories, to the detriment of companies and individuals you may have never heard of but who are just like you.

We also now have the internet and social media, where everybody's opinion becomes amplified, whether on Twitter, Facebook, Instagram, Snapchat, or whatever the next place is to go online, find others who agree with an opinion, and band together to go after companies or individuals they dislike. For those people, it feels *good* to receive information and regurgitate it in their own way—especially with a little keyboard courage, sitting behind a computer with the anonymity of the internet allowing people to act differently than they would in person. And because of social media algorithms, their beliefs are reaffirmed. No matter how far outside the mainstream their stance, all they hear is similar opinions from like-minded people.

On the other side of that online mob is the person or business owner those people come after, sitting there wondering what the hell is going on.

Sometimes there are people out there doing shitty things that should be, for lack of a better word, "canceled." But the large majority of people are just going about their daily business, doing what they've always done, thinking they're doing the right thing, and then they're blindsided. Their entire life is disrupted. And they are usually completely unprepared.

The problem with cancel culture is that the ultimate goal of these people is to ruin the life of the person being canceled. It's not just to get them fired or to shut down their business; it's to make sure they can *never earn another dollar*. They want to completely destroy their target.

If you're Harvey Weinstein, then sure, you've got this coming. But if you just crack a bad joke on Twitter, they'll come for you. Actress Kristy Swanson found that out when she was hospitalized for pneumonia and people *wished she would die*—and sent her messages saying as much—all because she previously supported Donald Trump.

Unfortunately, that's the world we currently live in.

Some of you may be thinking, "Sure, I've heard about what happened to Dave Chappelle and Joe Rogan, but the woke mob's not coming for *me*!"

All of us, whether we like it or not, are living public lives. As Andy Warhol said, "In the future, everyone will be world-famous for fifteen minutes." The potential exists for you to be very famous in a very negative way. Whether misjudging how innocuous that Facebook post is, assuming that difficult situation in a doctor's office isn't being recorded, or believing that the clubs you affiliate with, the church you go to, or the political beliefs you have won't impact your bottom line and ability to provide for your family...in this environment, all of these examples are possible places for cancel culture to come for you. None of us are immune.

Take the "anti-work" subreddit, for example, where employees post not only business conversations and discussions about how to improve working conditions but *anything* a boss does—for example, buying a new car while any of his employees work for minimum wage—which leads to calling him a piece of shit and him getting canceled.

Cancel culture is trickling down from giant corporations, politicians, and celebrities to business owners, managers, principals, and cops. Where does it go from here? Canceling your coworker because you don't agree with them?

We all have that crazy grandparent or uncle whose rants are pretty far outside current thinking. But the fact is that if anyone filmed most of us just saying what we think around the kitchen table, we'd end up canceled, too. In our current cultural space, everybody has an opinion, and everybody else has a cell phone that can instantly broadcast to the twenty-four-hour news cycle. At any moment, something you do in your everyday life can make you internationally infamous. In the blink of an eye, you can be on the front page of Reddit or the Drudge Report.

Because of this, *everybody* needs to watch their back. That's a scary thought, but I'm not just saying it to scare you. I see it happen every single day, and that's why it's so important for you to be prepared.

IT'S BETTER TO KNOW THIS
AND NOT NEED IT…

The information I'll share with you in this book is like having car insurance. You don't want to get into a car wreck, but if and when it happens, you'll be glad you were prepared. The time to buy that insurance, however, is not immediately after getting into an accident. You buy it ahead of time so you have that protection plan in place when something happens.

And here's the thing: this car wreck is inevitable, if not for you then for someone in your life. Without this suite of strategies, you're going to be as vulnerable as any person you've seen on late-night news or in that latest Reddit or Facebook post.

Although you wouldn't buy car insurance from the side of the road after getting in an accident, if you are already experiencing the worst effects of cancel culture, there *are* things you can do. Look for callout boxes like this throughout the book to give you additional examples and immediate information you can apply.

When you're going through it, I want you to know that you're not alone. This is a function of our culture right now, so this stuff is going to touch you; it's inevitable. But just know that there are two paths forward. Either way, it's going to be tough, and it's going to suck, but at the end of one path, you learn how to deal with shit, become mentally stronger, and survive...or you can make this a whole lot harder on yourself and potentially put yourself out of business—or worse.

Think about it. What would you do, right now, if a crisis were to hit?

I've seen people who are in the midst of getting canceled for saying something stupid, when the mob is out there trying to take away their business and ruin their life, and that person's first instinct is to call a lawyer. They think there's a legal process to all of this. But a lawyer isn't going to know that by tampering with the situation, you may actually make it bigger. They're trained in the court of law, not the court of public opinion.

Cancel culture was impacting politicians way before it reached the general public. Because of my work with those political clients, I have the experience, knowledge, and acumen to deal with these crisis scenarios. While a typical public relations or marketing professional, or even COO at a corporation, may be great at selling widgets or tickets to a park, they've likely never experienced anything that involves this much hate, vitriol, and negative attention.

People's gut instincts about how to deal with these situations are often the opposite of what they should actually do. As another example, in response to a social media post going viral, many people want to continue to post, to try to explain the content coming under fire. But that just draws the ire of everybody who was hating on that first post and exacerbates the harassment.

You are (probably) not a PR professional. Your response is likely not the correct response, and sometimes it's just as insensitive as whatever you said to get yourself canceled in the first place. And, hey! I'm not here to judge. My point is that a normal individual in this space will almost always choose the wrong strategy for the scenario at hand.

So whether you picked up this book because you recognize the need for insurance, or you are already going through it, you're taking the right steps because you realize that something needs to be done. That puts you in a better position than most people because you recognize that you need or will need help, so you need to learn what to do and not to do.

THE PHASES OF A CRISIS

I have thirteen rules, or guidelines, to help you prepare for or escape the situation you may find yourself in when the shit hits the proverbial fan. These rules are designed to help you through the phases of a crisis.

Let's first look at the phases of a crisis, and then I'll show you how my thirteen rules apply to those phases.

A crisis moves through six distinct phases:

- **Preparation:** There are steps you can put in place *before* a crisis even hits to be prepared ahead of time. (Even if the crisis has already hit, you'll still want to start here.)

- **Damage:** Whether the damage is self-inflicted or comes from external sources, you want to minimize the fallout to the extent possible.

- **Analysis:** You have to determine what the problem is, where the threats are coming from, and whether or not you need to respond.

- **Response:** Decide whether you need a response and, if so, what form it should take. (And if you and your team determine that a response is not necessary, what should you be doing now?)

- **Containment:** There's still work to be done after the response; the crisis is not just going to go away. If the response phase is when you call in the fire trucks, the containment phase is controlling and putting out the actual fire.

- **Recovery:** How do you recover from a crisis and rebuild your brand?

And here's how the thirteen rules for surviving cancel culture and other crises fit into those phases:

- Preparation
  - Rule #1: Be Prepared
  - Rule #2: Have a Team in Place

- Damage
  - Rule #3: Talk to Attorneys, but Not Too Much
  - Rule#4: Know Your Battlefield

- Analysis
  - Rule #5: Measure What Matters
  - Rule #6: Formulate a Plan

- Response
  - Rule #7: Move Fast
  - Rule #8: Own It and Apologize or Double Down
  - Rule #9: Know and Label Your Opponent
  - Rule #10: Get All the Facts Out Before They Do

- Containment
  - Rule #11: Don't Feed the Trolls
  - Rule #12: Move On

- Recovery
  - Rule #13: Rebuild the Brand

As you read more about each rule, I want you to be aware that these are not all hard-and-fast, step-by-step rules. I don't deploy all of them in every situation I'm called in to manage. Think of them instead as tools in a toolbox. Every scenario is different, so you want to have many tools to pick and choose from.

Conveniently, each of these rules corresponds to a chapter in this book. Over the next thirteen chapters, I'll lay out all of these tools so you know what they are and how to use them when necessary.

But first, I want to tell you a story—a *fishy* story—that I will continue throughout each chapter of this book, using it to demonstrate how each of those guidelines can be applied when necessary.

Yes, this story required every tool in the box. In fact, you might even call it a *whale* of a tale...

THE DAY THEY CANCELED SHAMU

SeaWorld is one of the first major instances of online cancellation that most people may recognize, even if they don't know the full story.

> Throughout this book, I will be telling the story of how we saved SeaWorld. But when I say, "*We* saved SeaWorld," I want to be very clear that I am talking about the entire team, including SeaWorld's internal team, not just my company. This was a united effort under the amazing leadership of SeaWorld CEO Joel Manby.

SeaWorld has always been a target of animal activists and PETA, who protest any animals being kept in captivity (yes, even house pets). These same radical activists came for Ringling Bros. and Barnum & Bailey, which ended up shutting down. They do crazy shit, like laying in front of the Capitol in Styrofoam trays, covering themselves with blood and plastic to say, "Don't eat meat." (They even want baseball teams to stop using the term "bullpen" because it's cruel to cows!) That online mob has always been there, but prior to the incident we're about to discuss, it had always been limited to a small number of people taking it to the extreme. It never reached the mainstream because people *enjoy* going to SeaWorld.

But SeaWorld became a much wider target in 2013 after a documentary called *Blackfish* detailed the death of a trainer, Dawn Brancheau, who was killed by a six-ton orca named Tilikum. The creators of that documentary knew how to appeal to a mainstream audience, saying that Tilikum went crazy because he was kept in a swimming pool instead of the ocean, so he acted out by killing his trainer. The theory they presented was that if the killer whale hadn't been in captivity, none of this would have happened—with no mention of the fact that he was an apex predator with the word "killer" right in the name!

Blackfish, which was picked up by Netflix and became one of their highest-rated documentaries, started trending. Suddenly, people saw it and started thinking, "Well yeah, those giant killer whales *shouldn't* be kept in tanks."

After the documentary was released, SeaWorld stock was sent spiraling, ending up still down 33 percent after a year. Park attendance declined by 17 percent, and profits dropped by *84 percent*. As the attack continued, the company was in turmoil. They were ready to start mass layoffs. Because of their cancellation, SeaWorld was in an existential crisis and on the verge of collapse.

There's currently a trend of believing that if your product is good enough, your voice is loud enough, and you feel justified in your position, you may be able to somehow subvert being canceled. But as you can see from SeaWorld, no one is too big to fail—not even a killer whale.

Because their traditional public relations and advertising folks weren't experienced in handling a crisis of this magnitude, SeaWorld's communications director, Jill Kermes—who was the former comms director for governor Jeb Bush in Florida—recognized that this was not temporary, not just a fluke that the company could rebound from. She said, "This is not a marketing fight; it's a political fight—and we need a political team to help us."

That's where we came in. All of the cancellations you see in society and on the internet have a political angle, so the response needed to come from people with political experience. And this was back in 2013 and 2014, so it was one of the first instances of a corporation feeling the heat from both the twenty-four-hour news media and the digital mob—things that political candidates deal with every single day.

I'll walk you through our specific strategy and show you how it followed each of the thirteen rules in the chapters to come. For now, suffice to say that over the first several months after we came onboard, and in the years since, we were able to develop a plan for SeaWorld that not only told their story—the *true* story—but was also able to beat back some of the online vitriol they were experiencing. It took creativity on our part to come up with the plan and discipline on SeaWorld's part to enact that strategy.

But now, years later, it doesn't take a documentary and an internationally renowned organization like PETA to get you canceled. These days, all it takes is somebody with a cell phone recording, retweeting, or screenshotting your words. That's the new *Blackfish*.

This is happening now on a mass scale. Whether you're Facebook, Google, or a mom-and-pop bakery, these types of situations land in the twenty-four-hour news cycle and are retweeted and posted to Instagram all day long. Everybody is getting a taste of what happened to SeaWorld in 2015, but what you need to know is how to come out the other side.

CHAPTER 1

BE PREPARED

**"Reason shows there is nothing either
good or bad but thinking makes it so."**

—Seneca

An example of how *not* to handle a crisis is perfectly illustrated through a situation that happened in my home state of South Carolina more than a decade ago. At the time, Mark Sanford was the governor, and he had a bright future ahead of him. In fact, there was serious talk about him being a contender for the Republican presidential nomination to run against Barack Obama in 2012. He was one of the most sought-after Republicans in the nation.

But that all ended in 2009 in a span of six days that shook the political world.

The governor disappeared on the Thursday before Father's Day. It didn't take long for rumors to start around the State House in Columbia. After a day or so, his wife told the Associated Press that he was "writing something and wanted some space to get away from the kids."

His spokesman, Joel Sawyer—a friend of mine from our college days—said Sanford had told him, "I'm not going to be here next week. If anything comes up, you handle it. I'm going to be hard to get in touch with." He hinted that he was going hiking on the Appalachian Trail.[1]

This is what Sanford said, but in fact, he was flying to Argentina for a tryst with his mistress.

By the day after Father's Day, what would ultimately become a media firestorm was just beginning. Where was the governor? His car was found at the Columbia airport, and all his outdoor equipment was in the back seat, so it was clear that he wasn't hiking. Eventually, a reporter named Gina Smith from *The State* newspaper tracked Sanford down, catching up with him at the Atlanta Airport just after he landed on a flight from Argentina. He rambled to her about his love of the Appalachian Trail and how he liked the adventure trips he'd been on over the

---

1 For my full-length interview with Joel Sawyer about Governor Mark Sanford, see episode 5 of my podcast, *Under Fire*, from May 7, 2021: https://open.spotify.com/show/1LDm6cKCTXbOh8ODAZ0zDg?si=KsuCjr9rRXSlyPw2OOVxMg&nd=1

years—Turkey, the Greek Islands, and various parts of South America. A staff member drove Sanford back to Columbia. He called a press conference a few hours later.

It was a moment that called for effective crisis communication.

With members of his team around him, including Joel Sawyer, the governor stood before reporters. The idea was for him to come clean, to rip the Band-Aid off. In a crisis, instead of the steady drip, drip, drip of information, he should have focused on getting it all out there in one fell swoop—the good, the bad, and the ugly all at once—but as briefly and concisely as possible. He *should* have kept it to "I lied. I wasn't on the Appalachian Trail. I was in Argentina with a woman. I was unfaithful. I'm sorry to everyone I've disappointed, first on the list being my wife and family." Then exit the stage.

The problem was that Mark Sanford was totally unable to say anything briefly or narrowly. He stayed center stage far too long that day, going on and on about everything from hiking to Bible study. He eventually got around to confessing his affair, but there was no strategy, no speech—just blabbering driven by his emotions.

Then, inexplicably, he took questions.

A few minutes later, as Sanford continued to dig a hole for himself, Joel Sawyer stepped in and grabbed him by the arm, encouraging him to drop the shovel. And, mercifully, the press conference was over. Time to move on.

As fate would have it, Sanford was given the greatest gift one could ask for in the midst of intense media scrutiny: a bigger news story. Michael Jackson died suddenly, shocking the entire nation. *Everyone* was talking about it.

But instead of letting his story burn out, Sanford threw gas on the fire.

Sanford gave a long stream-of-consciousness interview a few days later, describing his mistress as his soul mate. I'm not sure what Sanford was thinking, but a reporter got him to spill his guts. He talked about his feelings, completely throwing discipline out the window as he divulged details about how their relationship began and grew. All the while, he was damaging any hopes he may have had of putting the whole thing behind him and getting back to the business of governing. Ultimately, his career was mortally wounded.

As I tell my clients, "I can save you from outside forces, but I can't save you from yourself."

DON'T DRAG IT OUT

I see these kinds of situations happen with celebrities and politicians all the time. Instead of having a plan to say only what is necessary, they react emotionally and make their situation a whole lot worse. If Sanford had been mentally prepared, and if he had really thought about what was happening, he would have realized that it could have been a much smaller story and one that disappeared far faster.

One of the things I talk about with clients is what I call "the one-day story."

Clients sometimes freak out about an item in the newspaper or on the six o'clock news, overreacting because the story is about them or their campaign. Their uncle or grandfather or cousin calls them, and they immediately jump to the conclusion that everyone has seen the story. They panic and leap into full spin mode. But typically, not a whole lot of people have actually seen it.

That's why you have to wait and see how many people are aware of the story. The fact is there are other things going on in the world. Your crisis may end up being a one-day story because another crisis bubbles to the top. It could very well be no more than a hit everyone will forget about tomorrow.

Probably the greatest example of how one story can overshadow and minimize another dates back to the weekend of July 18–20, 1969. Late on that Friday, Senator Ted Kennedy drove his car off a bridge on Chappaquiddick Island in Massachusetts, killing a young lady named Mary Jo Kopechne. Of course, this would have been a monumental story any other time, but that weekend is also when Apollo 11 landed on the moon and Neil Armstrong took that one giant leap for mankind.

Being overshadowed by the moon landing—ironically first proposed and envisioned by Ted's older brother, President John

F. Kennedy—bought the senator time to circle the wagons and come up with a way to manage the story.

Ted Kennedy went on to a long career and was lauded as "the Lion of the Senate" after he died in 2009, despite the fact that he was responsible for a death and its effective cover-up.

But you never know if another moon-landing story is going to come along and bump your crisis out of the news cycle, so how can you make sure that you don't make your situation worse than it already is?

Do what the British do: *Keep calm and carry on.*

KEEP CALM AND CARRY ON

This uniquely British phrase is compelling because it speaks of being completely prepared to face and weather a coming storm.

When you're in the middle of a crisis, you are already in the fog of war. That makes it difficult enough to make good decisions, but when you let your emotions run wild, you're not making decisions based in reason.

Most people freak the fuck out, get defensive, and start responding in a way that's going to get them in more trouble—just like Mark Sanford did. They try to explain themselves, which leads to getting attacked more, and then they respond even more, until the entire situation spirals out of control.

In fact, the vast majority of people thrust into a crisis are just going to make the situation worse.

We have a fight-or-flight mechanism built into our bodies, over hundreds of thousands of years of human evolution, stemming from living in the wild, dealing with apex predators. That same reaction causes you to feel panicky and your heart to race when you get in trouble. It causes you to react quickly and instinctually rather than rationally.

The fact of the matter is our biology is not built for the twenty-first century and all of the new challenges it brings. When faced with a crisis, it's important to calm down, think it through, and find your mental footing so you don't act like your inner Neanderthal.

You are going to find yourself in a crisis. It's likely going to come from the cancel culture movement. You're going to think it's unfair. You're going to think your whole world is falling apart. You're going to want to scream and maybe even cry. But you have to *chill out*. Staying calm is the key to poise in the most intense and pressure-laden situations. Panic always compounds a crisis.

Around 90 percent of the time, the advice we give people is "Don't do anything." But that's hard to do when you're facing that fight-or-flight instinct. If you can't do nothing, however, you're likely to only make things worse.

So when you are emotional in the fog of war, how can you make the right decisions? By being prepared.

Let's compare the reactions of two mayors after the George Floyd protests in May of 2020.

In Minneapolis, as the protests turned to active riots and the city was burning down on live TV, Mayor Jacob Frey was nowhere to be found. When he did make media appearances, he was often crying and seemed so clearly in over his head.

Melvin Carter, the mayor of St. Paul, on the other hand, was visible, articulate, and well spoken. It was a contrast of epic proportions.

Being prepared means being mentally prepared as well as having a plan in place. That preparation then becomes your foundation so that when a crisis hits—and remember that it's not a matter of *if* but *when*—all you have to do is enact that plan (which will be even easier with some practice, as we'll also discuss later in the chapter).

GET FIT BEFORE THE CRISIS HITS

It's easy to say, "Stay calm," but it's a lot harder to actually do. The question then becomes: How does one stay calm?

When it comes to dealing with a crisis, the first rule is *be mentally prepared*. This is vital because there is always a crisis nearby.

You're either in one, waiting for one, or you've just emerged from one. Crises are not the exception—they are more like a rule. And the current cancel culture has created more kindling for potential firestorms. Get used to it.

We don't talk about this much, but mentally weak people falter and make things worse than they need to be. Without mental strength, people can't see the forest for the trees, and they basically lose their fucking minds. Mentally strong people, on the other hand, have the discipline necessary to make it through a crisis because they don't freak out or let their emotions control them.

Honestly, this is not just about mental preparation; it's also about mental *toughness*. I like to compare times of crisis to endurance events. I am a hardcore and avid endurance athlete. I not only run marathons but also ultra marathons, which can be fifty miles or longer, and I've finished two Ironman races. I listen to what David Goggins, author of the *New York Times* bestselling memoir *Can't Hurt Me*, says: "Do what is hard!" I compete in many triathlons because doing hard things toughens up the mind.

Goggins also talks about how physical work puts calluses on our hands, making them tougher. He says we need to do the same thing with our minds if we want to reach our real potential: "The only way to move beyond your 40 percent is to callus your mind, day after day. Which means you have to chase pain like it's your damn job!"

And the only way to prepare your mind is through exposure therapy. In psychological terms, exposure therapy is when psychiatrists try to get people to confront their fears by exposing them to the things they are afraid of. This is the same concept: Expose yourself to mental trials, to things that make you tougher so you can callus your brain.

A tough mind is prepared for a crisis. I think this is why I have also studied Stoicism. I love what Marcus Aurelius, the Roman emperor and Stoic philosopher, said: "The mind adapts and converts to its own purposes the obstacle to our acting. The impediment to action advances action. What stands in the way becomes the way."

In the first century, another Stoic philosopher named Seneca said, "Difficulties strengthen the mind, as labor does the body."

Basically, the idea is that taking on tough things enables you to do tough things. As the Navy Seals say, "Embrace the suck!" It goes back to this idea of finding comfort in the uncomfortable. Work isn't always fun. It's called work for a reason. You don't go on vacation every day; you go to work.

And a lot of times, it sucks.

I like to embrace the suck. If I'm running a marathon, and I'm on mile twenty-two, I dig deep. I might think, "This sucks, man. It's awesome to be in this pain." That mental attitude calluses my brain and creates strength. Every time I'm in a hard situation, it's making me a tougher person who can deal with difficult things.

It's making me a better person. It's making me a stronger person. Strong people are forged in the suck.

So I do endurance events, read Stoicism, meditate twice a day for twenty to forty minutes, all so that my mind is prepared to take on tough situations and react with logic and strategic thinking rather than mere emotion.

But don't just take my word for it. The late Kobe Bryant woke up at 4:00 a.m. every morning—even on game days. He didn't stop when he got tired; he built resilience. He pushed harder and harder on a regular basis so that when he was in the final quarter and the game was on the line, he would be used to the pain and could avoid fatigue.

In other words, he embraced the suck.

YOU'RE NOT AN EXPERT—BUCKLE UP

In addition to becoming more mentally prepared, you also want to be prepared by having a plan in place.

Cancel culture and crisis communication planning is a lot like home crisis planning. My family, for example, has detailed plans about what to do in case of an emergency. We have a fire plan. We have a tornado plan. We have a home invasion plan. And because we live on a fault line, we even have an earthquake plan.

All of these plans are written out, and we practice them as a family so everyone knows exactly what to do. (As you'll learn in the next section, practicing a plan is another important way to be prepared, by *reinforcing* that plan with practice.)

Without a plan in place, if you smell smoke or hear alarms going off, you're probably going to run around like crazy. You and your spouse will be bumping into each other, and you won't know where the kids are, who is helping them to safety, or even if everyone is out of harm's way.

But if you put in a little work ahead of time, by having that plan already drafted, you're not going to freak out when something happens because you know what to do. You're mentally prepared, and even when you're woken up suddenly and your heart is racing, you'll be able to take a step back and stop freaking out.

Easy enough to say, right? But how do you actually plan for a crisis in today's cancel-culture world?

The first thing to do is list out what *could* happen. Under each scenario, write who would be impacted as a result of that scenario. Then consider which players from your team you need to involve or what areas of expertise you need to acquire in order to mitigate your position in that news story. (In Chapter 2, we'll look at why you should have a team already in place.)

Let's say that you are a baker who owns the most amazing bakery in your town. You are the best damn baker around, but you are a *baker*. You are not a lawyer. You are not a public relations expert. You are not a communications expert. In fact, you are like the vast majority of Americans who have an area of expertise that lies outside of what is needed to successfully handle a crisis.

As a professional baker, you are already prepared for certain disasters: you have fire sprinklers and insurance for the bakery. You know that if a fire does break out, you're going to do X, Y, and Z.

(Similarly, most people know that if they drive regularly, at some point in their lives they're likely going to get into some sort of a car accident—probably a small fender-bender, where they know immediately to go to the glove box, find their insurance card, and call the insurance company.)

But what do you do when you accidentally end up in the spotlight?

Cancel culture is the new fire. It's the new car accident. Now you have to know what you're going to do when something different happens. What will you do if someone leaves a Yelp review saying that you called them the N-word? Whether you actually said it or not, that review is going to go viral. Someone copies it from Yelp, posts it on Facebook, and suddenly it has ten thousand shares. These days, that scenario is far more likely to happen than the fire.

Think through some of these possibilities ahead of time, and you'll be ahead of the game. Most people assume that the fire is probably going to happen to them at some point, but they *never* think they are going to become a victim of cancel culture. But as I keep reminding you, everybody has a phone in their pocket. What if one of your employees says something rude to a gay person? Not only will people assume the comment is *because* that person is gay, but the next thing you know, the internet will blow up with, "This establishment hates gay people and employs homophobes!" Suddenly, the entire LGBTQ+ community is boycotting your bakery—or, as in the case of the baker who refused to make a gay wedding cake, it could go all the way to the US Supreme Court!

I'm guessing that baker never thought he would become a national story, disrupt the entire country, and end up receiving death threats. (Even if you think through as many possible scenarios as you can, you can't think of everything!) You are never going to intend to wake up and offend the entire country; that's not how cancel culture works. Instead, you'll be going about your day, doing whatever you normally do, and the wrong thing will slip out of your mouth in the wrong place at the wrong time.

Think of Billy Bush and the interview with Donald Trump, where a hot mic caught the future-president saying, "Grab her by the pussy." Billy Bush was just interviewing the guy, but because he didn't immediately slam Donald Trump—a guest on his show—in the moment, he ended up getting canceled. He certainly didn't have any intent of going out there and doing that that day; he was just trying to be a professional and do his job!

Cancellation by proxy has run rampant. The way your employees interact with your customers can and will impact you as the business owner, so you have to think through your response and how you would react in that scenario.

I can't tell you what specific scenarios you might face, which is why I first advised you to start practicing mental preparation. Even though I don't know the details of your life and the potential crises you could encounter, I *do* know that you can learn to react appropriately so you don't make the situation worse. You can learn to sit on your emotions, meditate, practice mental toughness, and *do nothing*.

You can also envision what crises or potential areas for cancellation exist for you, and then you can begin to make a plan for exactly how to respond in each of those scenarios.

The time to act swiftly will soon be upon you (and we'll talk more about moving fast in Chapter 7), but haste makes waste, and you don't want to step in it and make things worse before you have a solid plan. The only way to do that is to gather yourself and be prepared, the same way you plan ahead by having car insurance, flood insurance, or fire insurance.

SIMULATION THEORY: CANCELED

It's not only important to have your plan in place long before a crisis hits, but it's also important to practice your plan. Whether it's your family practicing how to escape your house in case of fire, a public school running a drill for a weather or terrorist crisis, or a major corporation going through a mock public relations disaster or cyber attack, practicing your plan is crucial to success in case of a real crisis.

Crisis simulation—it's important.[2]

A crisis simulation involves an exercise where a fictional scenario is presented to a team to gauge its ability to effectively follow a plan prepared beforehand. During such a simulation, those in specific roles are tested for how they carry out their responsibilities as laid out in the crisis plan.

These exercises are used by a wide range of organizations from law enforcement to business to politics. In his crisis masterpiece *Failure Is Not An Option*, former NASA Flight Director Gene Kranz wrote:

The problems thrown at the controllers and the crew by the simulation supervisor prepared them for the real crises that might come in any phase of the mission from launch to splashdown. Simulation attempted to make events that could happen in real-time—malfunctions in any one of the many spacecraft systems, trajectory problems, or failure in the ground systems— as realistic as possible. With hundreds of possible malfunctions

---

2   For a detailed discussion about crisis simulation, listen to the *Under Fire* podcast, episode 14, "Preparing for a Crisis" with Stephan Merkens: https://open.spotify. com/episode/5XA4HhTyVC31F6ki6n2ap1

and many time critical mission events, the training opportunities are limited only by the hours and weeks available to train. We stimulated every phase under a variety of normal and emergency conditions.

Even high school students can do a crisis simulation based on the Cuban Missile Crisis at the International Spy Museum in Washington, DC, putting themselves in the roles of President Kennedy, Nikita Khrushchev, Fidel Castro, and their leadership teams, as the world was on the brink of destruction in October of 1962.

Some corporations spend months creating scenarios, building them to be as real as possible. The scenarios are done in a closed-loop system, where they can emulate Facebook, Twitter, YouTube, search forums, video blogs, and everything else a company may have to factor into their crisis response. They walk through a scenario with printed social media reports. They monitor email communications. They take cell phone numbers and have role players on the outside who imitate angry moms, activists, reporters, politicians, and others—all happening in real time.

There are also ground rules they put into play in these scenarios, including things like not communicating with the outside world for at least four hours following a crisis. It's like being in a war room or a debate prep for a candidate. The idea is to test operational strength.

Observations made during such exercises help identify potential weak spots in a plan—the kinds of things that are better to know and deal with before a crisis rears its ugly head.

If you're a small business owner, however, and it's more or less a one-man show, it's hard to practice all of these scenarios, but you can always practice calming the fuck down.

A WHALE OF A MISTAKE

Let's return to our SeaWorld story from the introduction.

SeaWorld didn't let their emotions control them. Instead, they made a different—nearly fatal—mistake: they never considered the fact that anybody would see them as anything other than the good guys. They let their own misperception of themselves, their own *arrogance*, keep them from being properly prepared.

PETA had been coming after them for so long that they believed that nobody was listening to those crazies. They thought they were too big to fail.

In fact, SeaWorld knew ahead of time that the documentary was coming out, and they sat on their hands. They weren't prepared for it in any way, and ultimately, they were blindsided by the reaction and the ensuing outcry.

But I know that you're not going to be like SeaWorld. You're going to get mentally tough, think through possible scenarios ahead of time, so you can make a plan and practice that plan.

However, you probably can't do it all on your own. That's why you need a team, and Chapter 2 will show you just why it's so important to have that team in place *before* the crisis hits.

HAVE A TEAM IN PLACE

"No matter how brilliant your mind or strategy, if you're playing a solo game, you'll always lose out to a team."

—Reid Hoffman

More than two decades ago, a supertanker was on a run from Alaska to Long Beach, California, carrying more than 53 million gallons of crude oil. Very early in the journey, the vessel hit Bligh Reef in Prince William Sound, and more than 10 million gallons of its cargo spilled into the water. The name of the vessel is etched in our collective memory—the *Exxon Valdez*.

Exxon did not have a crisis plan in place, so the best they could do was react to what would become a major environmental crisis.

Decisions were made on the fly with no real planning. The company's strategy was initially more about cleaning the spill than taking responsibility.

But they had time to put a crisis team together because the story unfolded over several days and even weeks.

You won't have that kind of time.

TELL ME WHO YOU'RE WITH;
I'LL TELL YOU HOW CANCELED YOU ARE

In these days of social media and viral communication, you may have only a few minutes to respond when a crisis hits. Otherwise, you're playing a game of catch-up from the start. Putting a team together is a vital part of preparation, as we looked at in Chapter 1. A crisis team is another form of insurance—you want to have it already in place *before* you need it.

You need to have your team in place ahead of time because you are going to have to make an assessment about your situation. You likely won't know if you may be civilly liable, criminally liable, or neither, so you need to talk to a lawyer. And if you don't already have one on retainer, you want to know who you would turn to in that scenario. You can't just call your tax attorney or your divorce lawyer. (We'll look at who else should be on your team in a later section of this chapter.)

I hate to even think about this, but I've recently begun putting together the plan for what should happen if I die. As awful as it is, I view it as a form of crisis preparation.

I compete in Ironman races. What would my wife, Elizabeth, do if I had an accident and drowned during a race? How would she access resources she needs? How could she get money from life insurance? How would she access our money in the stock market or invested in crypto?

Well, she knows that if I die, she should call the attorneys, our finance guy, and the crypto guy who knows how to get the keys to those accounts. After that, she should call my business partner Phil, because he'll help with anything else. This is the right team for that scenario—the people who understand what should happen and who will help her with the logistics while she handles everything else, including our three kids.

Without that team, my wife may eventually be able to get all the information she needs, but it would be much harder, and she doesn't need things to be any more difficult when she's in a crisis situation.

Let me be clear: nobody likes thinking about any of this. No one wants to think, "Someday I'm going to be canceled," or "Someday I'm going to die." It *sucks* to think about, but the reality is, at this point, one is just about as inevitable as the other. Like we talked about in Chapter 1, you embrace the suck and make a plan ahead of time so that a bad situation is not made even worse when it does happen.

In 2021, Colonial Pipeline was hacked and suffered a major data breach. Their 5,500-mile oil pipeline was not only their most valuable asset; it was also critical to America's economy.

But Colonial Pipeline Company already had a plan—regularly conducting drills for how to handle crisis situations—*and* they also had their team in place. They have a local communications office in every state where they operate, which allows them to have boots on the ground almost immediately when called for.

Of course, they had dealt with crises many times—things like small leaks or breaks—but never before had they faced something of this magnitude. And never before had anything risen to the level of a potential public relations nightmare. But the company responded quickly, demonstrating complete transparency, and although it was the worst crisis the company had experienced since its establishment in 1961, they became a model for how to handle a crisis.

A REALLY BAD SITUATION CALLS
FOR REALLY GOOD PEOPLE

Equally as important as having a team in place is making sure that you have the *right* team—one that has voices worth listening to.

The moment Joe Wilson screamed, "You lie!" at President Obama during his first joint session of Congress, all of us on his legislative and campaign team knew we had to take action.

Immediately, we put together a team to start capitalizing on that moment, and ultimately we helped him raise more money online than anyone else ever had up to that point.

But we didn't raise the money just because of what Joe Wilson yelled—we raised the money because of what Joe Wilson went on to say. He apologized to both the president and to Speaker Pelosi and admitted, "This is not what a gentleman does. I'm sorry, it was an outburst, and I shouldn't have done it."

Despite that apology, Joe Wilson was still attacked all over TV. They even tried to censure him in Congress. And we raised all the money off the fact that they didn't accept his apology.

We put together a team quickly: I was handling fundraising emails, and I hired a guy named David All to manage blogger outreach because I couldn't handle it all myself. We also had an internal communications team, and between all of us, we were able to raise $2 million in the course of a week.

We were only able to break that digital fundraising record because we reacted so quickly, and we were only able to react so fast because we had the right team in place, and we knew who needed to be on that team.

Corporations get most of their advice from marketing agencies, the majority of which are located in big cities and dominated by one side of the political spectrum. In today's cancel culture world, these companies need to realize that they are not in a marketing fight; they are in a *political* fight, and as such, they need to hire political help—from all parts of the political atmosphere so they're able to get advice that reaches the majority of Americans.

I see a lot of corporations responding strictly to the "woke" left and *not* responding in a way that attracts everyday middle Americans, because those corporations are getting their advice from big agencies out of New York and LA. You need people that understand *all* the people you are trying to reach. You can't just cater to California; you also need to talk to folks in Nebraska, Oklahoma, South Carolina, and Florida.

When you hire public relations professionals, they come with their own biases; they come from their own bubble. The best professionals in this business are the ones who take things into consideration from all sides of the aisle. They have a keen under-standing that their opinion may not be a public opinion. And they use facts and data to help you make decisions rather than based on their whims or feelings.

When asked if he would endorse Democratic North Carolina Senate candidate Harvey Gantt, Michael Jordan famously said, "No—because Republicans buy sneakers, too."

That kind of mentality shows the tightrope you have to walk in today's political climate. It really does take an expert to help you through that process, because you're not going to know the polling numbers or all the nuances to your messaging. In fact, most of the people you'll talk to don't have that political training and mindset.

The Difference between a Mountain and a Molehill? Perspective

Not only do you need to consider your messaging and mindset, you also have to take into account your audience—the people who buy your product or pay for your service and, thus, affect your livelihood.

When people like Green Bay Packers quarterback Aaron Rodgers (who misled the public about his vaccination status before catching COVID-19); actor, comedian, and podcast host, Joe Rogan (who used racial slurs on past episodes of his podcast); or comedian Dave Chappelle (whose comedy special *The Closer* included jokes about trans people) react to their inevitable cancellations, their strategy is necessarily different than yours should be, because they have different platforms and audiences than you do.

If your gut reaction is to say, "Screw this, I'm just gonna say whatever the hell I want 'cause that's how Joe Rogan does it," you're likely to get yourself into a lot of trouble. Joe Rogan, Dave Chappelle, and Aaron Rodgers can say a lot without it affecting their livelihoods. You probably don't have the same leeway. (Unless you also have an audience of 15 million people, like Joe Rogan. Then say whatever you want! Otherwise, you can't just go by the celebrity examples you see in the media.)

And that brings us to my next point: you need people on your team that can give you better *perspective*.

As soon as a crisis pops up, immediately and inevitably, everybody is going to want to be on your team. There are going to be too many voices, not all of which will have your best interests in mind, and not all of whom will be experts in this subject matter. Typically, the more voices you have around you, the less you actually hear.

One of the things I suggest to people is considering who would be in your "kitchen cabinet." No, I don't mean the place you store your pots and pans. Who are the people who calm you down, whose opinions you respect most? Who are the people who understand you and your intentions the best? Who would you be most comfortable sitting around your kitchen table and solving problems with? Choose one or two of them, just regular people, to be your sounding boards.

You are too close to the situation, so you can't see the forest for the trees—even if you are able to remain calm and mentally prepared. When you are in this position, it's nearly impossible to determine how to react appropriately. The single biggest problem I see is that people are so close to their own situations that they either think the world is burning down, so they run away or react impulsively and emotionally, or they think that everything's fine—and if it's fine, it'll all blow over, so they just don't address it. Those

are the two typical reactions, but they represent
the two extreme ends of the spectrum when the
answer often lies somewhere in between.

Rely on your team to provide a
more objective perspective.

If you're sounding off and texting everybody you know to get
their opinions on your situation, chances are you're going to get
bombarded with opinions and still not receive any good advice.
Limit your circle to your most trusted people, and then work
your decision tree to find the people who are best in their specific
areas of expertise.

Have you made the nightly news? If so, you need someone
with public relations experience to make the connection between
you and the reporters. You're not going to know how to reach
those reporters—or even which reporters to talk to.

Is it going viral? Is it a social media problem? If yes, find somebody who handles social media. Or at least have their number
so that when something happens, you can quickly reach out and
rely on them to help you in that scenario, especially if it's not
your strong point.

Every business at every level is going to have different calibers
of teams, but everybody can be prepared by making sure the people they're talking to are a small, close group of the people they

trust the most, including a public relations expert, a social media expert, and a lawyer.

No one needs to go through a crisis alone. It's not smart to try to handle any life crisis by yourself. That is a recipe to raise it to the level of trauma, so you want the right people around you, those who can help you deescalate the situation.

The NRA was scheduled to have a convention just three days after the Columbine, Colorado shooting in 1999. The convention was booked in Denver, just miles away from where the shooting took place.

Toward the end of 2021, tapes were released of the NRA's war room conversations about how to proceed, how to handle the media, and whether or not to cancel the convention. These conversations included their CEO, their executive director, their lawyers, their top lobbyists, their in-house PR team, as well as an outside PR team they hired specifically to help them come up with a game plan for getting through what would have been an existential crisis for them. They saw the importance of having their team in place ahead of time but also knew to bring in outside help when necessary to get help from the best people for the specific circumstance.

BUILDING THE TEAM

Disaster preparedness and response often conjures up familiar media images of a scene of devastation and governmental response—men and women associated with everything from local fire and rescue to gigantic federal agencies.

Though the US government seldom gets high marks for effectiveness and efficiency in how it does its business, there are rare bright spots where they seem to have figured a few things out. One example is something called the Incident Command System (ICS). Developed more than fifty years ago, it is a model for command, control, and coordination in response to disasters—wildfires, air or ground transportation accidents, wide-area search and rescue, traumatic weather events, and so on. Think FEMA.

The ICS is organized around five elements:

- Command
- Planning
- Operations
- Logistics
- Finance/Administration

Importantly, the command's director is always part of the executive staff in a particular response, which shows how vital an on-scene director is to ultimate success when dealing with an emergency. What I like about the ICS is that it's organized around five elements and not the exact members of the team.

The exact members of your crisis team will be completely dependent upon the situation. Being lampooned on *Saturday Night Live* is a lot different than a ransom hack of your customers' private data. Those situations will require different skillsets.

I can't give you an exact playbook here, but I can give you the key elements, which must answer the most immediate questions:

- Who is in charge?
- Are we in legal trouble?
- How bad is the public perception of our situation?
- How much will this cost?
- What do we do?
- What do we say?

Command: Someone has to be in charge. The buck has to stop somewhere. It could be the CEO, the Chairman of the Board, or a noncorporate client like a politician or celebrity, as long as someone in the room can serve as the final decision-maker.

Legal: You need to immediately know if you're in legal trouble, whether criminally, civilly or both. Staying out of jail is top priority. (The whole of Chapter 3 is dedicated to this topic.)

Polling: Is the situation as bad as you think it is? Is it a whole lot worse? Decisions must be made based on numbers, so you need someone constantly measuring public sentiment. (See Chapter 5 for even more information.)

Finance: Everything in life is about money, and crisis is no different. Make sure you're making the smartest financial decisions by having your finance team at the table.

Crisis Expert: As discussed earlier in this chapter, you need someone who can see the forest through the trees. An outside, experienced crisis team is a must.

Communications: You could have a lot of different audiences and a lot of different communications staff: PR, social media, internal, investors. You don't need them all at the table. Pick a communications leader to help develop the overall message and manage the media infrastructure.

Keep the team as small as possible. Too many cooks in the kitchen will cause confusion and delay action. I recommend having no more than eight people in the room.

Most importantly, have this team in place *before* the crisis hits. You should already have identified which teammates encompass each element. That way when the crisis is upon you, you only have to determine which elements are most important. You may not need all of these people in every situation, but if you have each teammate in place, you have your bases covered.

There's also something to be said for who *not* to have on your team. You want people who can offer differing opinions when needed, but there's no room for jockeying for position or playing games in a crisis. Think of the teams the Roy's assemble in *Succession*: they have horrible human beings around them. It doesn't matter what kind of great team you've assembled, if you put self-interested people or individuals who will exacerbate the situation around you, then you're being led down the wrong path. Anybody throwing that kind of shit into the mix needs to be taken off the team immediately.

Your crisis team needs to be a well-oiled machine composed of people who can disagree in the moment but ultimately come up with a great solution.

A Well-Oiled Political Team

In 2020, the incumbent Republican senator from South Carolina, Lindsey Graham, faced a tough challenge for reelection from Jaime Harrison, who had served as chairman of the South Carolina Democratic Party. This was despite the fact that no Democrat had won a statewide election since 2006.

My company was hired to handle digital and television media strategy. Though Graham had a decisive lead over Harrison in the polls at one point, things changed when money from outside the state began to flood into the Democrat's coffers. Democrats from around the country started rallying around Harrison. In fact, the Harrison campaign brought in more than $57 million between July and September alone, breaking national records. (The previous fundraising record in South Carolina was just $8 million.) This was the kind of money usually reserved for presidential campaigns.

It was a potential game-changer that seemed to happen overnight, and we had to react fast. We did. In fact, we quickly started matching Harrison dollar for dollar.

How?

We had a team in place. Senator Graham didn't have to spend several weeks recruiting a crisis team. He knew exactly who the players were. He had the best campaign manager in the country—Scott Farmer—as well as a fundraiser, pollsters, a media and social media team, and a digital fundraising team. Of course, our social media team had another fifty people working with them. Same with the other teams, including Campaign Solutions, the digital fundraising team. Each of them had many more workers. But we couldn't have all those people on conference calls. Scott wanted just five or six key team members participating in each conversation.

And because the team was small, we were able to react to the crisis quickly. We were able to put together a strategic plan in a short period of time and raised our own historic amount of money—more than $100 million. All because we were able to react to the crisis at hand so quickly.

By the way, Lindsey Graham beat Jamie Harrison by more than ten points in November.

SOMETIMES YOU NEED A PRO

SeaWorld called us just in time.

The people who ran SeaWorld thought they were immune from crisis because they were doing good work. Important research. Rescuing animals. Rehabilitating animals. And then releasing those animals out into the wild. They were sure everyone loved them and what they were doing, even though many of their efforts were not really known at all in America. They saw themselves as the heroes. How could anyone hate a company committed to saving our oceans and marine life?

The SeaWorld team could not see the forest for the trees. They were too close to the situation. And they mistakenly assumed that everyone thought of them as they thought of themselves.

Still, they tried managing the situation themselves, and that was a huge error. Outsiders are always better in crisis situations because they are not as emotionally close to what's happening. People who are too close have difficulty acting strategically.

SeaWorld waited an entire year following the release of the film before doing anything. That's when we (Push Digital) were brought in. Of course, by then, SeaWorld's attendance, approval rating, and stock had already plummeted, and it seemed like it would be impossible to ever bring those numbers back up to their pre-*Blackfish* highs.

Had we been working with SeaWorld at the time *Blackfish* was released, we could have helped them mitigate the fallout. But at least they recognized that they needed help from an outside team and brought us in to repair what damage we could.

Now that you know you need a team and who should be on the team, we're going to look more closely at one specific team member: your attorney(s). Chapter 3 will show you why you should definitely talk to attorneys...but not too much.

TALK TO ATTORNEYS, BUT NOT TOO MUCH

"Good lawyers worry about facts.
Great lawyers worry about their opponent."
—Harvey Specter in the television show *Suits*

The name Dr. David Dao might not ring a bell for you, but you likely remember what happened to him on April 9, 2017. The doctor had just settled into his seat on United Express flight 3411, flying from Chicago O'Hare International Airport headed to Louisville, Kentucky, when he was told that he was one of four passengers randomly chosen to be bumped from the overbooked flight to make room for four airline employees.

He refused.

What happened next was captured on a video that went viral: Dr. Dao was seen being forcibly removed from his seat and dragged down the aisle by his hands. He was on his back, his body was limp, and his mouth was bleeding. He suffered a broken nose and lost a couple of teeth in the process.

This created a PR nightmare for the giant airline. There was an immediate backlash, and the company's stock plunged nearly 4 percent as the video reached more than 300 million views on the internet. The White House webpage received a petition with 100,000 signatures in one day alone, demanding a government investigation into the incident.

By all accounts, the airline fumbled the ball in its response— or, more accurately, *failed* to respond—to what became a public relations disaster. The company's CEO, Oscar Munoz, took too long to issue any kind of public statement. When he did, it was one of those nonapology apologies. He didn't even come close to using the simple key word *sorry*. Then, in a letter to United employees (that was inevitably leaked to the media), Munoz blamed the victim.

This is a case where the PR cost was far higher than the legal cost. Ultimately, United Airlines paid Dr. Dao a settlement of $140 million, but the hit to their stock cost the company $1.4 *billion*.

Ever since this incident occurred, United Airlines has been cited as a compelling example of how *not* to deal with a PR crisis.

What *should* have happened in the immediate aftermath of Dr. Dao's dramatic exit from flight 3411 is that the company should have stepped right up to take full ownership. They should have immediately acknowledged that the incident shouldn't have happened and that they were conducting an internal investigation into the employees responsible. They also should have reached out to Dr. Dao right away to cover his medical bills and any other pain and suffering, and publicly demonstrated that they were taking immediate steps to make something very wrong right.

So why was a big company that should have known better so sluggish and ineffectual in their response?

One word: attorneys.

GOOD LAWYERS KNOW THE LAW;
GREAT LAWYERS KNOW THEIR ROLE

In Chapter 2, we established the importance of having a team in place ahead of time so that you are prepared before a crisis hits. One of the members to have on your team is an attorney, though you may need more than one attorney, or if you don't actually have an attorney on retainer, you should at least know who you would consult.

You want to secure that legal advice when needed, because who cares about public opinion if you're going to jail? Staying out of jail is always priority number one. However, outside of that, an attorney's advice is not going to help you against a cancel-culture crisis. There are disciplinary differences between swaying the court with a legal decision versus the court of public opinion, and attorneys are just not suited for the latter.

> Consider the Streisand effect: a blogger once put Barbara Streisand's house in a photograph online, and she hired a lawyer to get them to take down the picture. The blogger did so...and then told the rest of the world about Streisand hiring a lawyer, which then propelled the photo of her house to the rest of the internet, where far more people saw it than they likely would have from just the initial blog post.

And that's why I say that you need attorneys on your team, and they have to be one of the first people you talk to, but beyond that, take their advice sparingly.

The most common advice from an attorney is "Don't say anything." But taking that advice can often land you in PR trouble. Your lawyer is trying to protect you from jail or a large cash payout, but there are other fates that are also horrible, for example, a viral public relations firestorm that undermines your business. The reality is that you could lose multitudes more money in the court of public opinion than you would in a court of law.

That's exactly what happened with SeaWorld. They waited an entire year before responding to Blackfish, mostly on the advice of their attorneys, who advised them not to say anything because they were concerned about their court case.

SeaWorld's attorneys and marketing teams told them not to respond...so they didn't. They went silent for a full year, thinking, "Hey, we're the good guys. We save animals. Everybody loves SeaWorld. They're not going to believe this crap!"

The resultant hit to their stock prices, park attendance, and reputation, however, was way worse than anything that could have happened in court.

Additionally, attorneys slow down the process of responding to a crisis, and that's by design. In their world, the more you delay, the more time you have to craft your response (not to mention racking up those billable hours!) If you lean on an attorney in a noncriminal instance, you're sacrificing time, and (as you'll learn in Chapter 7) time is often the one resource you're never going to get back. You'll never get another shot at those first twenty-four to forty-eight hours of a crisis, and if you've eaten up all that time with analysis paralysis with your lawyer, who knows how much money you've lost or damage to your reputation is taking place.

LEGAL ADVICE THAT SHOULD BE ILLEGAL

Prior to reading this chapter, you may have thought lawyers were only there to keep you out of jail and financial trouble, and they are. But too many of them try to build themselves up as marketing experts, as well. When lawyers are in a position to start influencing, or even dictating marketing strategy, they can actually put your enterprise at risk.

Many, if not most, CEOs seem to view lawyers as the be-all, end-all of problem solving. But their opinions have to be weighed with the perspectives of those who actually know something about public relations. You should definitely listen to PR professionals during a PR crisis, especially if their advice differs from what the lawyers are saying.

Many of the instances we're seeing in cancel culture are about politics and reputation—they have nothing to do with the law—but nevertheless, we often see lawyers attempt to insert themselves into those situations, when that really isn't their area of expertise. Use the right expert for the job. As a public relations professional, I wouldn't try to represent somebody in a court of law.

As another example, in 2012 the South Carolina Department of Revenue was compromised by a phishing scam that wound up exposing the personal information of millions of people, including financial data and even Social Security numbers.

Governor Nikki Haley handled the matter very well, but the state's legal team made sure that everything was fully vetted by both state and federal law enforcement to avoid compromising the investigation. Of course, they also didn't want to do anything to inadvertently hinder any possible recovery of the data.

In a crisis, most politicians love to say things like "I promise you we will take steps to ensure this never happens again." The problem here is that law enforcement professionals who deal with cybersecurity will tell you that approach is a mistake. It actually invites hackers to try again and to do so with even more sophisticated and damaging methods.

Attorneys like to control the narrative, and they think that in speaking up, their clients are going to find themselves in more legal trouble. So they often give advice that anything you say can be used against you. But in this day and age, when things can go viral in a moment, sometimes saying nothing is the worst possible thing you can do.

HOW TO DETERMINE WHEN
YOU NEED AN ATTORNEY

The question to consider in a crisis is "Am I legally responsible in some way?"

That can be broken down further into two questions: "Am I civilly liable for something?" and "Am I criminally liable?"

If the answer to either is yes, you need to talk to an attorney. And, yes, you may need to talk to an attorney to determine the correct answers to those questions in the first place.

In fact, it's almost always a good idea to talk to an attorney first. If they determine that you have a criminal issue, take that attorney's advice. If it's a civil issue, then you have to weigh the potential civil outcome versus the potential PR outcome to determine how much you're going to listen to your attorney as compared to your PR team. If you have no criminal or civil liability at all, you can keep the attorneys in the room to cover your ass, but you should only listen to your PR guys when making strategy decisions.

The attorneys you may need to call on in a crisis are civil attorneys, contractual attorneys, regulatory attorneys, political attorneys, and ethics attorneys. But again, their law degrees and experience don't always translate into great PR strategies.

WHEN YOU LAWYER UP, YOU SLOW DOWN

When the British Petroleum (BP) Deepwater Horizon oil rig exploded in the spring of 2010, not only did eleven men lose their lives, but in many ways, the Gulf Coast region was changed for the long term. Of course, it was also a major PR disaster for BP. They handled matters poorly, responding slowly and playing too much of a blame game.

The company's lackluster response was largely driven by attorneys who wanted to shield them from lawsuits as best they could. As a result, BP's CEO, Tony Hayward, who had cut the PR budget shortly before the explosion, acted too late and did too little—a mistake that ended up costing the company more than $60 billion in legal penalties (criminal *and civil) and cleanup costs, in addition to the 51 percent stock drop that cost $105 billion loss in value.*

The company's failure to control the narrative is a textbook example of the importance of a company-wide public relations plan.

It was much the same with a more recent case—the fitness brand Peloton. You may remember that in 2021 the company recalled its highly popular treadmills in the wake of a series of reported incidents involving injuries and the death of at least one child. Their response to the crisis was sluggish, and they missed the opportunity to make things right with their customers. Acting on the advice of their lawyers, they took time to weigh out all of their options. In the end, the delay only compounded Peloton's problems with consumers.

Lawyers play a vital role in your business, but they are best used when they stick to what they know. There are certainly times when an attorney's advice is wise in a crisis, but you have to determine when to follow that advice and when to turn to someone else on your team.

Another important element—and the fourth of our thirteen guidelines—is to know your battlefield. Crises start and spread on the internet, and it's not your daddy's dial-up. Chapter 4 shows you how the web has changed and what *you* need to know about its effects on cancel culture.

KNOW YOUR BATTLEFIELD
(SPOILER ALERT: IT'S THE INTERNET)

**"The Internet is so big, so powerful
and pointless that for some people it
is a complete substitute for life."**
—Andrew Brown

The internet can be used for ill or good. Take the case of
Nikki Haley and how I accidentally jump-started her career.

It all began with an internet show called *Pub Politics*
that I was hosting back in 2010 with my Democratic col-
league, Phil Bailey. The premise of the show was that we'd drink
with a politician, staffer, or lobbyist and talk shop. It was a free-
wheeling kind of thing. On June 2, 2010, just a few days before

South Carolina's primary election, our guest was Jake Knotts, a Republican member of the South Carolina State Senate.

At the time, Nikki Haley was a little-known member of the South Carolina House of Representatives, who had been running for governor for more than a year. She was the ultimate outsider running against the system, a woman against the good-old-boy network. She had no shot of winning, but she was making noise.

So, it was inevitable that her name would come up on the show that night. Well, Knotts had a couple of whiskeys and a couple more Budweisers under his belt and was very, shall we say, *animated*.

Referring to Barak Obama and Haley respectively, he said, "We already got one raghead in the White House. We don't need another in the governor's mansion."

This was, of course, a derogatory and racist reference to Haley's Indian-American ethnicity. Knotts continued to dig the hole deeper, talking about Haley's parents, how her mother wore a ruby on her head and her father wore a towel on his.

The internet began to blow up *before* the forty-five-minute show was even over. The next thing I knew, I was being attacked for not standing up for Nikki Haley, but in the moment, I was so shocked, all I could think was, "Hold on, did he just say that shit?"

The episode went viral globally, and it created publicity and sympathy for Nikki Haley, enhancing her outsider image. I took the video down, believing I shouldn't promote racist shit. She even used that to her advantage, saying the "good old boys" were protecting Knotts. Her poll numbers jumped about twenty points almost overnight. She received 49 percent of the vote in the primary a few days later, forcing a runoff, which she won handily. That November, she was elected as South Carolina's first female governor, capturing more than 51 percent of the vote.

Haley is a prime example of someone who benefited from the lightning speed at which information travels online.

THE INTERNET IS BIGGER THAN YOU THINK

The internet is a vital tool, and it helps us accomplish so many things. Although it has only been around for a relatively short time, it is hard for most of us to imagine our lives without it.

But we must never forget that the internet can also be a dangerous *battlefield*.

When I first started talking about crisis communication back in 2009, I had a thirteen-point presentation laid out, which I delivered in boardrooms full of stodgy old white guys who thought the internet was nothing more than family photos on Facebook and the headline on *Drudge Report*.

Back then, the internet was an important talking point because I needed to emphasize to those codgers the way things play out online and the speed at which information now circulates around the world, that something could go viral long before it ever appeared on CNN.

Even today, they don't understand the reality of the internet. They don't understand Reddit or TikTok. They may have heard of Twitter, but they don't really get that, either. They just don't see the way the internet actually works.

Now, of course, there are even newer technologies that many people are oblivious to. Take Reddit for example: Reddit is a social media platform completely unlike Facebook or Twitter. It is, to use their tagline, "the front page of the internet." It's where the internet starts. It's also where many cancel culture crises start because of the nature of the platform: people sharing news and insights, not what they ate for lunch. Many influencers scour Reddit to see what's coming up next.

But if you don't know the landscape of your battlefield, you would never know that Reddit exists or that a potential issue is bubbling up right under your nose.

Let's imagine a hypothetical scenario. A sixty-year-old corporate executive whose company makes shoes thinks the company is doing great, so he goes away for vacation. While on vacation, someone texts him the link to a subreddit accusing the shoemaker of underpaying their workers. The CEO blows it off, thinking, "I've never been to that website. It doesn't look relevant to me."

While he's away, customers start boycotting the company. Upon his return, the CEO has to deal with real-world complaints that feel like they are coming out of nowhere all of a sudden. Then he has an employee walkout as the employees connect with the local manufacturers' union. This becomes a local news story that makes it on Twitter. From there, a national news channel picks it up and does an investigative piece that discovers not only have they been underpaying workers, but they haven't been paying overtime. Now it's a legal *and* civil matter. CNBC picks up this bigger story, and the stock plummets.

All of these dominoes fall, bigger and bigger, because the person in charge didn't pay attention to something that seemed small and insignificant on a niche website that didn't make sense to them at the time, because they didn't know this battleground even existed.

Social Media Makes Everything Worse

It should come as no surprise that social media can create an instant crisis. Let's look at three different real-world examples of cancel culture blowing up online.

Aer Lingus's COVID Cancelation

When news of COVID first hit, Aer Lingus, the flagship airline of Ireland, said everything right. They were reassuring at every turn, telling customers and the public that they would respect and install all the best COVID-19 safety protocols—including social distancing.

However, on May 4, 2020, damaging images of a crowded flight departing from Belfast quickly went viral on the internet, causing an outcry on social media. The company responded quickly but poorly: "In light of the unexpectedly high loads on the Belfast-London Heathrow service this morning and the level of demand for the route, Aer Lingus is reviewing its processes and procedures applicable to the operation of this service." They added the predictable disclaimer, "The safety and security of Aer Lingus' customers and crew is our top priority."

The social media frenzy painted a different picture, one of the airline as a profit-obsessed brand that operated with a total disregard for client safety in pursuit of those profits. It took some time for the airline to reclaim its previously positive image.

Robinhood Robs Customers' Data

The case against Robinhood, a stock trading app that deceived clients into thinking it was a free-market trading app while selling customer data to the highest bidder, was made after a social media firestorm. Clients flooded Twitter and TikTok, and the story took on a life of its own. It eventually led to the company having to pay a $65 million fine.

Chris Pratt Acts Like a Prat

Trying to just be a "normal" person, on November 2, 2021, actor Chris Pratt used his Instagram account to share how much he loves his wife and daughter. His words were immediately taken out of context, and it blew up into a huge news story.

Let's take a look at what he actually said:

Guys. For real. Look how she's looking at me! I mean. Find you somebody that looks at you like that!! You know!? We met in church. She's given me an amazing life, a gorgeous healthy daughter, she chews so loudly that sometimes i put in my ear buds to drown it out, but that's love! She helps me with everything. In return, periodically, I open a jar of pickles. That's the trade. Her heart is pure and it belongs to me. My greatest treasure right next to my Ken Griffey Jr. Upper Deck Rookie card. Which if you know, you know is saying a lot. It's her birthday in about 6 weeks. So if I don't get her anything, I'll tell her to look back on this post. Love you honey. ♥ ♥

People complained that he was "objectifying" his wife or that saying he has a "gorgeous healthy daughter" with her was somehow a dig at his ex-wife, Anna Faris, or their son who has health issues.

Or—consider this—it *could* just be a man in love who wanted to show off his wife who he adores and who appreciates the life they have together.

In this case, social media is only partly to blame. Chris Pratt just didn't understand the landscape. He was using Instagram like you or I would, like he's just any other person, but that's not how a celebrity or someone in the public eye should use that medium. He forgot that some portion of his millions of followers would be looking to take the things he says out of context. Had he better understood the battlefield, he might have shared his thoughts in a group text to family and close friends rather than to the entire world.

AS THE INTERNET GETS BIGGER, YOUR PROBLEMS BECOME MORE NICHE

Not only is the internet a place where cancel culture can blow up, but the battlefield is changing rapidly.

People used to connect with their friends on Facebook and talk to the world on Twitter. Now, however, instead of trying to talk to everybody, people are narrowing down their groups to find people who are more like them. The internet creates niches where people can find communities of other people who share a common interest, connecting those who would otherwise never be connected.

Instead of going on Facebook and only talking to the few hundred people you've managed to connect with in your life, you can now virtually meet millions of people around the world and connect with your own like-minded groups on Reddit and other communities.

The anti-work subreddit is a good example of this. It was only six weeks from the first mention I heard of it to when it hit the *New York Times*. During that time, millions of

people connected to this one relatively small community—
something that wouldn't previously have been possible.

But why does this matter? Well, if you have kids (or spend
time around kids in any capacity), you are likely familiar with a
certain tactic.

The kid will ask his mom, "Mom, can I have dessert?"

Mom will say no. End of discussion? Far from it.

The kid moves on: "Dad, can I pleeeease have dessert?"

Dad says yes. Finally, the answer he wanted.

That kid was doing a simple version of what everyone on the
internet can do: opinion shopping. You can find people online
to support just about any opinion you can imagine—I mean
anything. And because battlegrounds are being drawn to support
those opinions, crises can bubble up from anywhere.

The battlefield is constantly changing. Part of knowing your battlefield is understanding that not only does this crisis spread at the
speed of light, but the internet itself is changing, too. To know the
battlefield is to constantly be paying attention to the dynamic web.

KNOW WHAT YOU DON'T KNOW

You do have to know and understand the ever-changing landscape of the battlefield, but that doesn't mean you have to become
an expert in social media.

If you have a team, you want to hire people who understand the ins and outs of how and where things happen online. In the hypothetical shoe manufacturer example I gave you earlier, the CEO should have turned to his team to determine whether the rumblings on the anti-work subreddit were something he could ignore...or, as it turned out, were something he needed to pay more attention to. (Ironically enough, the person with the greatest understanding in this area is likely to be the person with the least amount of influence, probably the youngest person in the PR department.)

But even if you don't have a team of people to help you through this, you can still gain a greater understanding of the internet.

First, know what you *don't* know. Don't make assumptions about how people are communicating; just because you don't communicate one way or use a certain platform doesn't mean other people aren't all over it. Understand that there are parts of the web you simply don't see, that there are entire conversations happening among niche communities on different platforms like Reddit, Anchor, Signal, and WhatsApp. And, for most of us, this is likely always going to be true: very few people know most of what's happening online.

The current iteration of the web is now heading toward private conversations, smaller niche communities, and greater activism. People form groups that get vocal about the things they care about. Not only can everyone have their opinions validated online, but anyone can become an activist online for either side of any cause you can think of.

I'll give you an example that many people probably don't have any idea about. In November of 2021, Paramount announced that it was cutting ties with Netflix so that it could air the entire *Star Trek* franchise on its new streaming service, Paramount Plus. The international *Star Trek* community raised hell because you can't watch the new season of *Star Trek: Discovery* unless you live in the United States.

Again, most people wouldn't know about this, but I'm in every *Star Trek* group you can be part of. These are passionate people around the world who, like me, dress up in costumes at conventions and spend thousands of dollars on collectibles. We're not talking about twenty people; there are hundreds of thousands—potentially millions—of international *Star Trek* fans who joined together to contact ViacomCBS and protest the change. But even with all those people speaking out, the general public isn't even aware this took place.

The larger point here is that these *Star Trek* fans are in these niche communities. Everybody has something they're passionate about, and they're not just on Facebook; they're in their own subreddits and Signal groups. That's the web today. Just because a discussion doesn't enter your area of the internet doesn't mean that it's not happening. And if you're not aware, it can blow up in your face.

BE AWARE, YOU'RE BEING WATCHED

So what's the answer here? Is it to stay off the internet completely, to never say anything so your words can't be taken and twisted? Of course not; that's not reasonable. Besides, even if you stay completely in your own comfortable little corner of the internet, someone else can still post about you and bring attention you never wanted!

I want you to understand that *privacy no longer exists*. Assume every interaction you have, whether in person or on the internet, is being recorded. Act as though every word and action you take is going to be scrutinized, because everything you say and do can and will be used against you in the court of public opinion—whether you put it out there yourself or not.

You may think you are really careful in all your Facebook posts, so you're fine, right? But everyone around you is walking around with a media company in their pocket, and every word that comes out of your mouth (or that gets posted online), even if it's a joke, can be taken the wrong way.

I have a friend named Liz Mair who is a political consultant. In 2021, she thought she'd post something funny on Twitter after a frustrating day trying to get her kid to eat: "I have resorted to burning Pokémon cards as a punishment when my kid doesn't do basic stuff he has to do."

It was just a joke, but it went viral, and Liz was ripped across the internet as this horrible mom, basically being accused of child abuse. But think about it: if you're a parent, what's more important to you than that, than being a parent? Literally nothing. And there's nothing worse than having your parenting criticized and your character as a mother torn to shreds all because of a joke.

Unfortunately, Liz didn't understand the battlefield. You can't crack those kinds of jokes. You have to understand that you are constantly being monitored, and if you are a leader or have any sort of authority in any way—as a cop, a local councilman, the leader of a company, hell even a *mom*—someone is always looking to take you down.

As the CEO of a small company, I've gotten to the point where I only talk about serious business issues with five people on my team. I let my partner Phil handle talking to everyone else in our staff, and I stick to asking how they're doing. Every word that comes out of my mouth is scrutinized, so I use those five people as filters to make sure that nothing I say can be taken the wrong way. When I write blog posts, I send them to Phil and ask him, "How is this going to be taken?"

And you can do the same. Get a second set of eyes on things. See how it comes across. Realize that the way you've always done business is not necessarily the way you can do business now.

You need a sounding board on your team for those sorts of decisions, but you also have to be self-aware about your surroundings and your specific business's landscape. That's not something

I can teach you in this book, but I can make you aware that some of the things corporations were able to get away with years ago will not be perceived the same way today.

Previously, a good CEO delivered profits to their shareholders. A good CEO today, on the other hand, is someone who pays their taxes and always follows the golden rule by treating employees the way they want to be treated. Your company may have always paid its employees X percent over minimum wage, and that was fine because there wasn't an outlet for complaints, but that's not the landscape we live in now. Years ago, that CEO might have been a dick to all their employees, and very few people would ever hear about it. Now, if you treat your employees like shit, the entire world knows about it instantly.

On both the personal and professional level, that angle of self-awareness is important to adjust to the realities of today's battlefield.

THE INTERNET IS FOREVER

At the beginning of this chapter, we talked about how Nikki Haley benefitted from the explosive speed of the internet. Now let's look at an example that shows the opposite.

The MLB made the decision to move its annual All-Star game from Atlanta, where it had been long scheduled, to Denver as a reaction (many would say an *overreaction*) to Georgia's new election law, legislation that President Joe Biden hysterically referred to as "Jim Crow in the twenty-first century."

Though few had taken the time to actually read and study the law, preferring to instead blindly accept the frenetic and dumbed down chatter on the internet and social media platforms, it created a potential firestorm for MLB executives. They had a massive knee-jerk reaction, one that wound up hurting tens of thousands of the people they thought they were defending. Officials in Atlanta said that more than eight thousand hotel reservations were canceled, and assorted Black-owned businesses that depend on baseball lost out on much-needed revenue to replace what had been lost to the COVID-19 pandemic.

Additionally, Denver has a Black population of just 9.8 percent, while Atlanta has a Black population of 34.3 percent. The MLB took the game from a historically important city in the Civil Rights movement, the home of Dr. Martin Luther King Jr., and gave it to lily-white Denver. In effect, MLB canceled itself, damaging its reputation in the worlds of sports and politics.

The speed with which all of this happened is proof-positive that the internet is a battlefield tailor-made for cancel culture. In pre-internet days, a successful boycott would have taken weeks to organize for maximum impact; today the world wide web can instantly turn a boycott into a flash mob.

This is exactly what SeaWorld experienced after the *Blackfish* documentary was released. People could watch the movie online, then find other people on the internet to voice their thoughts to and shore up their opinions. These people fed off each other's outrage until the wave of animosity toward SeaWorld seemed like it would overwhelm the parks.

Fortunately, as you'll soon learn, we were able to also use the internet to our advantage, sharing the *real* story about SeaWorld, going behind the scenes, and giving the world access to the good they put out into the world.

Unfortunately, there's not a lot you can do about the internet or the people on it. You just have to be aware of how it works and try not to become today's "main character."

A lot of people are going to read this and think, "Just be a good person and don't do anything shitty, and you'll be okay." (In fact, my two rules personally used to be: never compare anything to abortion or to Adolf. If you stay clear of those two things, you'll be okay.) But that's not the case anymore. If I'm walking into my office and a woman says, "Hey, Wesley, you look great today," and I reply, "Thanks! You look nice, too," I would assume that's okay; I'm not being a dirtbag. But no, that could be taken as sexual harassment.

The rule of "just be a decent human being" is gone. People are looking for reasons to be mad, so unfortunately, you have to assume that someone is trying to destroy you at all times. That is such a pessimistic view of the world, I know. But Liz Mair wasn't being a bad person; she was just cracking a joke about her kid, and now she's branded like that *forever*.

Because that's the other thing you have to remember: the internet is forever. Whenever someone googles you, your name is going to come up in conjunction with that bad joke you cracked—permanently. The internet doesn't go away.

Let go of the assumptions you may have had about the internet: that if you didn't see it on Facebook or Twitter, it's not a big deal, that they're only coming after politicians or celebrities, that jokes are no big deal, that people will give you time to explain, "That's not what I meant," and even that you can just be a good person and you'll be fine. Let go of all of that, and you just might make it out alive.

CHAPTER 5

MEASURE WHAT MATTERS

"Insufficient facts always invite danger."

—Spock

Whenever a product launch or change in a brand turns out to be disastrous, someone will almost inevitably bring up New Coke.

Back in 1985, Coca-Cola announced it was changing its flagship product, not to mention its secret formula, to a soft drink they said would be smoother and sweeter. Coca-Cola was number one in the soft-drink market at the time, but Pepsi was coming on strong. At the time, the CEO of Pepsi said, "These two products, Pepsi and Coke, have been going at it eyeball to eyeball, and in my view the other guy just blinked."

Actually, Coca-Cola did more than blink—it went temporarily blind.

People *hated* New Coke. Protest groups popped up (no pun intended!) with names like "Old Cola Drinkers of America." And seventy-nine days later—after thousands of angry calls per day and one Coke consumer even trying to sue the company— the president of Coca-Cola announced, "We're bringing it back, the original taste of Coca-Cola returns as Coca-Cola Classic and soon America will have a real choice."

The giant soft-drink company had made a big mistake. Their president went on to say, "The simple fact is that all of the time and money and skill poured into consumer research could not measure or reveal the depth and abiding emotional attachment to original Coca-Cola felt by so many people."

You can avoid becoming the next New Coke with one relatively simple tool you learned in school: you've gotta know your math.

AND THEN SATAN SAID,
"PUT THE ALPHABET IN MATH!"

Every decision you make during a crisis should be based on mathematical calculations that will show you the best way to go.

This is for the same reason you should bring in outside counsel: most people are typically too close to their situation, so they either think it's worse than it is (and throw gas on the fire, making it even *worse*), or they minimize it because they don't understand just how big it really is. Whichever side of the spectrum you fall on, failing to measure both the size of the situation and what your response should be means that you will not have an accurate assessment of the scope of the crisis.

Additionally, people often bring their preset assumptions about what they think they are going through. But when you're the subject of the crisis, you have zero actual perspective on what the crisis is. You can see neither the scope of the crisis nor its depth. This is why you need to use tools for a quantitative understanding. Numbers don't lie.

Starting from the beginning of a crisis, you first have to know: How big is the crisis? Is it really as bad as you think it is? Or is it worse? What are people really saying? And who are the people doing the talking?

Some comments may blow up with certain communities, but you have to consider whether that even matters. Are the people you actually care about going to be pissed...or is it just people who would be pissed off anyway? If something Donald Trump says goes viral and a bunch of Democrats talk shit about him, that's just another day. But if he says something that pisses off his base, then that might merit a response.

So much of the online conversation is just clutter—people who would never buy your product or vote for you. So using mathematical tools cuts through the noise and helps you figure out whose opinion really matters.

Math can also give you insight into how to formulate your response to a crisis if you determine that you do need to respond. What should that response be? What should your commercial show? What should your press release say? What should you tweet?

Math answers two questions for you:

- Should I respond?
- If so, how should I react, based on who is upset and what they're upset about? (Different audiences want to hear different things.)

From there, measuring the reaction to your response can show you how it's resonating. Is it working? If so, you may decide to put more money behind it. If it's not working, and favorability isn't changing, then you know that you need to change the message.

I've told you to know your math, but you may be wondering, "What math do I really need to know?" You need math that measures how people are feeling about the current situation and your potential response to it. Let's take a closer look at what that means.

WHAT DO YOU NEED TO KNOW?
(AND WHERE CAN YOU FIND IT?)

There are a few ways to measure reactions. Let's look at some definitions.

Polling: Polling measures public perception. It typically occurs over a few days, during which a large segment of the population is asked questions about an issue or crisis, giving you an overview of favorability. Through that poll, you can get what are called crosstabs, where you can dive into more specific demographics. Most people are probably familiar with the concept of polling from exit polls during elections, but you may not realize that corporations and politicians are polling all the time to measure what's happening on a daily basis, especially in the case of a crisis.

Tracking: Tracking is more of an immediate time capture of the situation, showing what happened overnight, for example.

Sentiment Analysis: Sentiment analysis measures the web and online conversations, using digital tools for language processing and text analysis to monitor and measure the conversation in real time, mainly over social media. You could, for example, go through and monitor the entire Twitter conversation around a crisis and get an analysis of whether the conversation about your situation is positive or not. Again, this can be done in real time, whereas polls typically take a minimum of forty-eight hours to turn around.

Twitter is really the best place to see real-time
sentiment analysis. You can perform some
sentiment analysis on Facebook, but a large
segment of that population has their profiles set
to private, so it can't be read. Twitter is also made
for short, fast responses, so you are more likely to
see people responding to events in real time.

Focus Groups: Focus groups are groups of people you get together and show a message to see whether or not they like it. You can have either wide swaths of people—Black people, white people, older people, younger people, parents—or you can have a specific audience.

Analytics: Analytics are the metrics of what is happening online. This is probably the measurement category the average person is most familiar with. How many retweets, shares, web hits, or Google searches is something receiving? Those can be indicative of whether something is worth responding to or not, and it can tell you the best way to respond, depending on which way the metrics are going.

If you are a large corporation, politician, or celebrity, you probably have a PR team measuring these things for you. But if you're a small business owner, you're going to have to perform some of this measurement yourself.

> There are plenty of tools that allow you to track metrics
> and perform analysis. Google Analytics is one you can use
> for your business's website; Zignal Labs is another.

If you receive a negative comment or something goes viral—if
a Karen comes into your store and calls you a racist—you'll be
able to see if she's just screaming into the ether and nobody is
listening to her (in which case, you can just ignore her). But if it's
getting thousands of retweets, and you can see the sentiment on
the comments is going a certain way, it can be indicative of how
you need to respond.

When Should You Start Measuring?

In episode 40 of *Under Fire*, we talked to Brent Buchanan, CEO
and founder of Cygnal and a pollster, about how to use polling
during a crisis.[3] He says that medium and large companies should
conduct polling *before* a crisis even occurs:

> The biggest [piece of advice] is don't wait until there is a crisis to
> figure out where you stand, because then you don't know who

---

3 The full recording of my podcast *Under Fire*, episode 40 with CEO Brent
   Buchanan, uploaded March 1, 2022, can be found here: https://open.spotify.com/
   episode/5Obcfv8W06CwLNW8BPA59u

you've lost. You simply know where the people stand at that moment. And it could be that this large group of folks that have always disliked you, and they like you less now than they did before. But it's not like they swapped sides, they were with you and now they're against you. And this is probably one of the biggest mistakes that companies, and even a lot of campaigns, make where they just don't invest in regular tracking to see how are we viewed, and how is that changing, and who is that changing with?

Because if you don't have that trend line, you don't know what in the world actually occurred when the crisis happens.

Politicians guide their actions to the polls because it's a statistically sound way of measuring where people are at. You get a baseline reading of a population's current stance, and then you can also measure how those feelings shift later.

One of the reasons we saw vaccine and mask mandates lifted in the spring of 2022 is because Joe Biden saw that public sentiment had shifted toward ending COVID restrictions rather than staying in crisis mode.

There are very few public crisis scenarios where polling and sentiment analysis aren't used—only if the audience is too small to be statistically valid or there aren't enough resources by which to conduct these types of surveys.

As another example, during the Black Lives Matter movement in 2020, there was a massive, two-day protest down here in Charleston, South Carolina, that pretty much destroyed King Street, which is the center of our tourist industry. We were polling for numerous state senators in the area in real time to see how people felt about this crisis. There were so many elements mixed in: Black people upset for legitimate reasons but also complete devastation, looting, fires, gunshots, and numerous people arrested.

Charleston has been named "the best place to visit" by Conde Nast for six years in a row, and our economy is driven by tourism. When that's devastated, it affects the lives and livelihoods of everyone in the city. The public was seeing peaceful protests on one screen and on the next seeing the Apple Store being looted of every single computer and device they had, and that was just one store! Scenes like this affected every aspect of our economy.

Analyzing public sentiment at the time allowed us to ask, "Are people okay with the fallout from these protests?" so that legislators could get their talking points in order as they were considering passing laws to restrict protests. The legislators were both in session in Columbia and running for reelection at the same time. They couldn't wait weeks to find out; they needed to know in real time, "Where is the public on this?"

Through polling, conducting phone surveys, and sentiment analysis, we determined that while people had empathy for the peaceful protesters, they were absolutely not going to put up with any protests that turned into a riot. The BLM movement caused themselves a lot of harm because people began to fear that any protest or anything public from BLM was going to turn into something that could completely devastate our economy.

LET'S WALK THROUGH IT

Now that you know what we're measuring, why to measure, and when to start, let's walk through an example of how each of these measurements are used.

When we first started working with SeaWorld, they had no clue how bad their favorability numbers were. Sure, they saw their ticket sales dropping and their stock tanking, but there were two important things they didn't understand: how people felt and how they should respond.

We needed to turn to the math machines.

First, we issued a large poll to thousands of people to try to find out how bad the crisis was. Some questions were:

- Have you seen anything bad about SeaWorld lately?
- If you did, did that impact your opinion of SeaWorld?
- Would it change your mind if you knew that SeaWorld is the number one conservation organization in the world?

We also polled them to see what they would think about us running a full-page ad in the *Wall Street Journal* sharing SeaWorld's plans to stop breeding killer whales in captivity.

Once we made that announcement and it was all over the news, SeaWorld's CEO appeared on *Good Morning America*. We tracked overnight to see what people thought about the announcement. We also performed sentiment analysis in real time while he was on TV. All of this allowed us to continue dialing in our response to be the most effective as we continued to address the crisis.

When CNN bought the rights to *Blackfish* and aired it over the Labor Day holiday weekend, we ran sentiment analysis to see what people were talking about during it.

Our digital ad response worked so well that we turned it into a television ad and aired it during the Winter Olympics. Before doing so, we showed the commercial to a focus group of middle-aged moms to see how it would be received. They were our focus group because that's who we were most trying to influence since moms are the primary decision-makers when it comes to where their families go on vacation.

> Whenever we show commercials during the Olympics or the Super Bowl, we are looking at the sentiment analysis on Twitter as they air nationally because people are talking about it in real time.

The math showed that the response to our ad campaign was amazing—so amazing that it was worth putting tens of millions of dollars behind it. You wouldn't want to start there, because you don't want to spend that kind of money with no guaranteed return on a response that isn't proven. But we were confident in our response because that decision was based solely on the math.

Measuring helps formulate an appropriate and proportionate response to an emerging situation. When it comes to crisis management, it's good to take a page from a carpenter's manual: measure twice; cut once.

But what can you do with all those measurements once the crisis hits? As you'll see in Chapter 6, the measurements you take form the basis of your strategic planning.

FORMULATE A PLAN

"There is a way out of every box, a solution to every puzzle; it's just a matter of finding it."
—Captain Jean Luc Picard

n December of 2021, Vishal Garg, the CEO of Better.com decided to fire 10 percent of his staff—we're talking about nine hundred people—on a Zoom call.

As he's telling these people en masse that they've lost their jobs on a call right before Christmas, he talked about how well the company was doing after a $750 million cash infusion. Then, as he fired them all, he said, "The last time I did it [fired a bunch of people], I cried. This time I hope to be stronger."

What a clown!

Better.com is a big enough company that they should have a PR team, and somebody should have advised Garg to handle it differently. But from the way it all went down, it's pretty obvious there was no strategic planning done at all.

And it doesn't seem like Better.com learned anything from this, either. In March of 2022, an additional three thousand employees received severance checks—*before* they were told they were being let go!

THE IMPORTANCE OF STRATEGIC PLANNING

Shakespeare said, "All the world's a stage." You are now an actor on that stage, like it or not. You have to realize that you can't be as open, transparent, and spontaneous as you may like to be because you have to act as though the whole world is watching. Therefore you have to rehearse—or plan—the role you're going to play.

In order to create a strategic plan in response to a crisis, you have to first know what the crisis is—or what may be coming. We'll discuss SWOT analysis, part of which helps to determine the threats you may face, in the next section. Here, it is important to point out that it is only by identifying those threats ahead of time that you can create and enact a plan to defuse them.

When threats are identified on the front end, so many crises can be prevented. Even for those you can't prevent, your response can be both faster and better with a solid plan.

When Jack Dorsey resigned as CEO of Twitter at the end of 2021, the new CEO, Parag Agrawal, received some flak for an old tweet from 2010: "If they are not gonna make a distinction between Muslims and extremists, then why should I distinguish between white people and racists."

Twitter's response was both rapid and appropriate, likely because they had already identified potential problems and planned a response ahead of time in case it became necessary (as it did). Agrawal had gone on to tweet *back then* that he was quoting from *The Daily Show*, and Twitter posted a glowing recommendation from Jack Dorsey to accompany that announcement that Agrawal would be taking over. People bought Agrawal's explanation, the letter from the previous CEO smoothed things even further, and now nobody gives a shit.

But Twitter likely didn't come up with that letter on the fly. High-level corporations vet their future leaders. They knew Agrawal was climbing the ranks, so once it became clear that he could potentially become the CEO, they did their research into him.

Corporations that don't do that—that don't look back at the public statements their people have made to find anything that could be hazardous and make a plan to address it—get caught unaware and thus are forced to *react* rather than being *proactive*. The people who are most crushed by crises are the ones who never see them coming in the first place. Those who are blindsided are the most devastated.

I'm not saying that you should live in fear, but you put yourself in a better position when you are realistic about the potential for crises on the horizon.

An example of this failure to plan is Jon Gruden, the former head coach of the Las Vegas Raiders. In 2021, it came out that he was talking shit about Black and gay people in the locker room, and accusations about these remarks had been made for years. Instead of only looking at his win record before naming him head coach, the hiring team should have researched those allegations and spoken with players and other people who have been in the locker room with him. It's no different from doing a background check and calling references when hiring a new employee.

Had the Raiders done their research, they would have discovered the accusations, or at least realized he was cracking some bad jokes, and they could have come up with a strategic plan for how to address the situation. (You've learned by now that it wasn't a matter of *if* those allegations were made public but *when*.) As it was, the Raiders had no response ready, and Gruden was fired.

The Raiders made two major mistakes here (other than hiring a racist head coach): they didn't determine the threats ahead of time, and because of that, they didn't formulate a plan for how to deal with them.

Let's look at what you can do differently so you can be less like the Raiders and more like Twitter.

DIGGING DIRT AND FINDING BODIES

You probably know that we do a lot of opposition research in political campaigns. All those negative ads you see on TV start out as notes in a large binder of documents compiled by a researcher. Everything—and I mean *everything*—about a candidate is in these binders. Obviously their political record is there, including every vote, every donation, every speech, and every public statement. Everything about their personal life is there, too. Financial records, arrest records, scholastic records, and information about their family. We even send "trackers," basically kids with cell phones, to chase the opponent around to hopefully get that perfect slipup moment that could go viral.

What you may not know is that we do the same for our candidate, too. This is called vulnerability study. Going into a campaign, we have to know as much, or even more, about our guy as the other guy. What have they said in the past? What have they tweeted or posted on Facebook? What are all of their interviews, their votes? Do they have a criminal record or liens against them? We must know all the threats, whether personal—like a divorce or arrests—or political—like votes, books, or past speeches. And we must know how hard those threats hit so we can be completely prepared for anything or anyone that could come after us.

We identify those threats by performing SWOT analysis. This is a technique used in strategic planning to determine the

Strengths, Weaknesses, Opportunities, and Threats for a business, project, or even an individual. Knowing the threats in particular, what could potentially be coming at us, allows us to prepare. If they drop X, then we know we're going to do Y. At all times, we're identifying what those threats are, because it's only by identifying what may happen that we can begin to plan for it.

Internal vs. External Threats

But this threat analysis isn't only useful in political campaigns. Corporations, small businesses, and individuals should also do the same. You may not have the same level of threat that a politician faces (and, thus, you won't necessarily need to do that same level of research), but you can still face attacks. Whether you have a team doing it for you or you're doing it yourself, there is some level of SWOT analysis you can do yourself.

Threats can be either internal or external. Examples of threats that a company might face externally include attacks from an opposition group, like PETA with SeaWorld, or accusations of using sweatshop labor for Nike. Internally, a threat could be something like the CEO drinking and driving, getting a DUI, and going to jail.

Internal threats include those you find from the background research, which could come out and result in attacks. External threats consist of the opposition coming after you, and they're always going to come after you if they can. So what are they going to find?

Try to identify your weaknesses. What are your internal threats? What are your external threats? In other words, what can they come after you for?

MAKE A PLAN BASED ON THOSE THREATS

Once you've done your research, the next step is to develop a plan for what happens if those threats become a reality, either to remove the threat or have a response ready in case anyone else ever digs up that information.

> Sometimes we even have ads already in the
> hopper, ready for when that attack comes.

If, for example, you have some questionable tweets from the past, once you've identified those as a potential threat, your strategic plan may include deleting those tweets and others like them, or even deleting your entire Twitter account.

But that may not always be the best strategy. If people have already dug up the tweets, you're going to get attacked for deleting them. So you have to do analysis. Is it better to delete it or to prepare a response to address it?

If you're not a big name, perhaps a candidate running for office the first time, you can likely delete the tweets, because it's unlikely that anybody will have captured them. But if you're a celebrity or well-known political figure, people will probably have already gone back and found those old tweets. At that point, you have to prepare a response, saying something along the lines of "This was taken out of context," or "I've completely changed my views." (Chapter 8 will give you more information about when to apologize and when to double down, and we'll take another look at whether you should delete or not in Chapter 11.)

You also need to recognize that there is zero separation between your personal and professional life anymore. Anything you say in your personal life will have an impact on your professional life. You can be fired (or your business can come under attack) for what you post on Facebook and Twitter—even if you only post on your personal accounts.

This is incredibly important to be aware of in a world that is so divisive. Everybody is angry, and it's all too easy to pop off a response on Facebook in that state. But you have to understand that your words can be used against you by your employer or a competitor. You have to strategically think through anything you put out there—past, present, and future.

The Threats You're Creating Right Now Are the Worst of Them All

In addition to looking for threats from your past, you have to be aware of the potential effect of your *current* actions. Strategic planning also has to account for what you're saying today, and as we established in Chapter 4, you have to think through everything you say on a daily basis. How can those words be used against you?

This doesn't only mean what you're saying out loud; it also encompasses everything you send in emails, post on social media—even how you act in public. We now have all these Karen videos going around. That is a direct result of the advances in technology, which give anyone the ability to record you anywhere you are. Assume every action is being recorded and act accordingly.

There has to be a level of strategic planning with every communication you make, and you have to assume that everything has the potential to come out.

> As I mentioned in Chapter 4, you should run social media posts by someone else and write down what you're going to say when you speak in front of groups of people rather than speaking off the cuff.

Each crisis is different and, therefore, requires a different response. The point is to start by having a plan in place. Know how to evaluate what areas of your business may be concerned and what you need to do right away. Then know who you need from the team you already have in place (as you learned in Chapter 2).

Keep It Simple, Stupid

There is a principle known as Occam's razor that says, basically, the easiest or most obvious solution or explanation is typically the correct one. That applies to crisis management, too. Typically, the simplest path to victory is the right one, and it's often the first one you come up with.

But that doesn't mean you need to move on it immediately. Get it down on paper, confer with both people you trust and people who don't share the same opinions with you about the plan, and *keep it simple.*

The simplicity of the plan is key. Like machines with too many moving parts, complicated plans don't work. They break down. So make your plan quick, easy, and avoid having too many moving parts so you can execute the best crisis strategy possible.

And, yes, you have to write it down. Here's why: In the midst of a crisis, inevitably, you'll jump on a conference call that will include you (of course), your team, your spouse, maybe your lawyer, your closest friend, and any personal assistants you may have. You'll all toss out a bunch of ideas, weigh pros and cons, and talk about next steps. A written plan gives you an after-action report. It says, "Here are the things we're going to do in sequence. And if we take these steps, the outcome should be X."

This doesn't *guarantee* an outcome, but it prevents you from skipping steps that are going to be crucial to the outcome you desire.

YOU GOTTA *SEA* IT COMING

SeaWorld was completely unprepared for the big attack from PETA; they never anticipated the threat, despite the fact that they were constantly under attack from activists. Maybe PETA had been a minor threat for so long, lobbing attacks they never won, that SeaWorld became complacent. Somehow, they just never saw *Blackfish* coming.

They didn't perform a true, thorough SWOT analysis.

Because they had been attacked by PETA before, they knew that PETA was a threat. What they *didn't* recognize was the internal threat. They never thought, "Oh shit, what if a killer whale kills a trainer?"

And it's that internal threat that enabled the external threat, PETA, which had been there all along just waiting for an opening.

The lesson from this is that you are your own biggest threat, and in the public view, you can be your own biggest enemy. In the past, you had to worry about other people lobbing grenades at you from the outside. Now, however, we've reached a point where you're already holding the grenade, and your attackers are just waiting for you to blow yourself up so they can get it on video.

There's an old political adage that is fitting: "Never interfere with your enemy when they're in the middle of killing themselves." The majority of the time in politics now, we can just sit back and wait for the opposition to do or say something stupid.

But that's why you're reading this book. Instead of being the person who hands their opponents an attack strategy, *you* are going to remove the threats you can and have a plan to defuse anything that remains.

And once you do, you are going to *move* on that plan—fast. Chapter 7 shows you how.

MOVE FAST

"A good plan violently executed now is better
than a perfect plan executed next week."

—George S. Patton

n November of 2021, while Travis Scott was performing at his
Astroworld concert in Houston, Texas, the crowd surged forward, leading to a "crowd crush," or stampede, that left more
than three hundred people injured, dozens hospitalized, and
ten people dead. Within minutes of this happening—literally,
while Travis Scott was still onstage—video of the event went
viral around the world.

Had Travis Scott (or his team) read this book, they would
have known what to do: he would have immediately left the
stage, pulled together his team, and figured out what was

happening. In doing so, they would have seen that there were actually two crises in play: the crisis on the ground as well as the resultant PR crisis.

Instead of handling either crisis, however, he and Kylie Jenner went to Drake's afterparty at Dave & Buster's. Travis Scott didn't even respond until after midnight—three hours after the crisis kicked off. Kylie Jenner responded the next day, and Drake didn't respond until Monday, after the entire weekend had passed. By then, people were talking about canceling Drake, Travis Scott, *and* Kylie Jenner. Additionally, LiveNation, who put on the concert, faces millions of dollars in lawsuits.

We'll look at some other steps Travis Scott and his team should have taken later in this chapter, but I can tell you now that instead of partying at Dave & Buster's, they should have had a response ready—and *fast*.

ACT SWIFTLY TO STOP THE BLEEDING

Mark Twain is attributed as having once said, "A lie can travel around the world and back again while the truth is lacing up its boots." But that was more than one hundred years ago—long before the internet of today. A lie can now get to every cell phone on the planet before the truth even opens its eyes.

Because of the speed of the internet, you have to respond immediately to any crisis, correcting a lie within minutes. You have to be prepared to move as fast as the internet does, because the internet doesn't wait on anybody.

> The military has elite rapid response teams that stand down most of the time, but the instant there's a crisis, they're already in motion to respond.

We're in this digital space now where if you don't respond immediately, everyone in the world is going to hear about it within minutes. You've already seen examples of how fast the internet moves in this book. In Chapter 4, I told you about my podcast guest calling Nikki Haley a "raghead." That comment was picked up by CNN and the *New York Times* before the livestream even ended.

Obviously, things happen faster than you can deal with them. And sometimes there may be nothing you can do to stop the spread, but you can minimize it and cut it off *if* you move quickly with an appropriate response. The first hours are critical because they can shape so much of the reaction to that crisis.

If you fail to move fast enough during the initial crisis, you risk letting the court of public opinion determine the outcome, and they won't let you make your case first. You also have to remember that an unchecked lie becomes the truth. If there's nothing pushing back on that lie, then that's what people are going to believe. (Sometimes even when you do push back, they won't believe you. It's all about what gets the most attention.)

An example of exactly that is the reaction to actor Alec Baldwin, who was holding a gun that went off and shot two people on the set for the movie *Rust*. Alec Baldwin didn't respond at all for weeks, and then he gave an interview to George Stephanopoulos to say, "It wasn't my fault, someone else handed me the gun, and I didn't pull the trigger."

It was made public that during that period of radio silence, he was in his apartment crying because he couldn't emotionally handle what happened. All the while, his reputation was ruined because he didn't respond, and now there's nothing he can do that would make that crisis better.

If you want another example, look no further than Robert Caslen, the former president of the University of South Carolina. In May of 2021, he gave a graduation speech in which he appeared drunk and bumbling, even referring to the school as "the University of California."

Video of his speech shot around the internet before he even left the stage, but Caslen didn't respond for two days. During that time, people kept watching the video and noticed that part of his speech sounded familiar. Ultimately, it was discovered to be plagiarized directly from a commencement speech given by Navy SEAL Admiral McRaven in 2014. Because he didn't respond to the initial reaction garnered by the video, the crisis compounded and grew bigger, leading to Caslen's resignation from the university.

While you are unlikely to end up in a situation like Alec Baldwin's, or even Robert Caslen's, let's look at the steps to take when—not if—you find yourself in your own moment of crisis.

STEP ONE: ASSEMBLE YOUR TEAM

The first step in any crisis is to *immediately* assemble your crisis team. (Don't know what that is or who should be on your team? Go back and read Chapter 2. I'll wait.)

In Chapter 2, I told you about the time Joe Wilson yelled at the president of the United States. Within the hour, we'd assembled our team. And only minutes after that, the chief of staff for Wilson's national campaign office was on the phone trying to determine the action steps to minimize the crisis. Just one example of rapid response done right.

STEP TWO: PLAY PR CHESS

The second step is to play PR chess. Not only do you and your team have to decide the next moves you're going to make, but you also need to figure out the likely countermoves. If you say X, what is your opponent going to say? If you don't have an opponent, what is the public going to say? And then what is your response to *that*? You can't just be thinking about your first move; you have to be able to see the entire board and know your next five moves.

One strategy that can be helpful in determining what your next move should be is to play a game I call "Best of All Worlds." First, ask yourself (and your team), "What's the best scenario that can happen from the outcomes of our actions? What's the worst scenario that can happen?"

The best-case scenario is your goal. Once you are clear on that, you can examine what steps need to be taken in the next twenty-four hours to move closer to that goal. Knowing full well that a single action will not get you to your desired outcome, instead look at what moves the ball forward. What will get you to the next goal post so you get the chance to fight another day?

If we look at what Travis Scott could have done differently, perhaps his goal should have been to appear empathetic toward the families of the people injured and killed at his concert. What actions could he have taken in the first twenty-four hours after the event in order to immediately express his empathy? Maybe he could have given a statement, posted on Instagram, or visited people in the hospital—anything *other* than slinking away to party at Dave & Buster's.

Thinking through the worst possible scenario, on the other hand, tells you what to avoid. It allows you to see where the pitfalls are so that when you try to move toward your goal, you don't actually wind up worse off than when you started.

If you don't have a best-of-all-worlds scenario—an end goal—to work toward and a worst-case scenario to avoid, you're left aimlessly making choices that send you in all different directions, with all different outcomes...not necessarily the one you want.

STEP THREE: REMEMBER YOUR MATH

Once you've determined your goal and the first step to take toward it (and maybe even the next step after that), you should immediately begin to measure the reactions to your response. (Again, if you don't know what I'm talking about, you should. This was the topic of Chapter 5, where you learned the measurement should start the minute a crisis happens.)

Think about it. The president has his national security council in the situation room. If there is a global event, he doesn't just hear about it, pick up the phone in the Oval Office, and say, "Bomb them." He goes to the situation room, where there's already a team in place analyzing information to develop a plan.

After Kendall gave his speech in *Succession*, when he flew off-script and named his father responsible for the abuses within the company, the first thing he did was get in the car and ask, "What's the public sentiment? What are they thinking about it?" The first team he hired was his digital team to start measuring what was going on.

This is a fictional example, but it shows what really has to happen in a crisis. You have to first determine how good or bad a situation is by looking online and seeing what people are saying about it in real time. That measurement will tell you if you actually need to respond.

STEP FOUR: RESPOND—*IF* YOU NEED TO

The final step is to decide if anything has to be done. Sometimes moving fast means figuring out if you need to move at all, and 80 percent of the time, you probably don't even need to respond.

Measuring tells you when you need to respond quickly or when you need to stand down. Get the team together, measure, and formulate a plan—one you could pull the trigger on immediately. But sometimes the plan is to just keep quiet. Other times it's to wait a day or two and measure to see if the story has legs or if it's going to die down or be eclipsed by another story.

You may be in a crisis that looks really bad for you, but then Elon Musk and Elizabeth Warren get into a Twitter battle that same day. Suddenly, no one's paying attention to your crisis anymore, so you shouldn't say anything that would draw their wrath back to you.

Following these steps means that when you respond—if you do—you won't be responding from an emotional place. And if you choose not to respond, it's because that's the best strategy, not because you're running away or sticking your head in the sand.

> SeaWorld waited an entire year after *Blackfish* aired to respond. By then, they had taken a huge hit, and we had to spend five years trying to repair that damage. If they had responded faster, I truly believe the fallout would not have been as severe.

BE LIKE PELOTON

A good example of a company handling a rapid response to a potential crisis is Peloton. (Perhaps they learned from the mishandling of their previous treadmill crisis.)

The *Sex in the City* reboot *And Just Like That...* depicted Carrie's husband, Mr. Big, riding a Peloton before (spoiler alert!) apparently having a heart attack and dying. HBO actually contacted Peloton and asked for permission to use their trainer on the show, but Peloton had no idea their bike would become a tool for this major plot point (which, as you will see, makes their response even *more* impressive). After the episode aired, Peloton stock dropped 11.3 percent.

But Peloton obviously knew what they were doing when it came to a crisis, and they knew how to move fast. Within a couple of hours, their response included a cardiologist saying that Big didn't die from riding the Peloton; he died from being a fatass who drinks all day. (I'm paraphrasing.)

Even better, within thirty-six hours, they cut and released a TV ad, produced and narrated by Ryan Reynolds, wherein Chris Noth, the actor who played Big, can be seen sitting by a fire, chatting with the trainer, asking if she wants to go for another ride. It ends with a voice-over by Ryan Reynolds extolling the virtues of Peloton's workouts and saying, "He's alive."

> Of course, they also had to move quickly a week later when Chris Noth was accused by two women of sexual assault. Peloton immediately removed the ad, and both Peloton and Ryan Reynolds deleted their tweets.

That is rapid response at its finest, coming while it was still in the forefront of people's minds. They inserted themselves into the conversation, with a response that was smart and cheeky and, most important, very, very fast. I've never seen a corporation move that quickly!

The team at Peloton clearly followed the steps laid out in this chapter. They had a team in place so they could consult about the best thing to do. They performed sentiment analysis, or other measurements, to know what people were saying about the episode. And when they decided to respond, they came up with *two* great responses—the cardiologist and the commercial—really quickly.

Peloton may have gotten some other things wrong and had shitty responses in recent years, but they absolutely nailed it with this one.

As we've discussed, sometimes you'll need to respond to a crisis and sometimes you won't. Sometimes you'll want to say you're sorry, but other times, you haven't done anything wrong, and you're ready to double down. Check out Chapter 8 to learn what to do in both situations.

OWN IT AND APOLOGIZE– OR DOUBLE DOWN

"It takes a great deal of character strength to apologize quickly out of one's heart rather than out of pity. A person must possess himself and have a deep sense of security in fundamental principles and values in order to genuinely apologize."

—Stephen Covey

Some great political leaders throughout history have shown the benefits to be gained by taking ownership and apologizing during a crisis.

In 1961, then president John F. Kennedy approved a CIA initiative for American-backed Cuban rebels to topple

Fidel Castro, the Communist dictator of Cuba. The Bay of Pigs invasion failed within days, leaving one hundred men dead and more than 1,100 prisoners in Cuba.

In a press conference, Kennedy accepted sole responsibility, saying, "Victory has a hundred fathers, but defeat is an orphan...I am the responsible officer of the government."

After his speech taking full blame—even though there was plenty of blame to go around—his poll numbers shot up because people respected his willingness to take responsibility for what had happened.

Similarly, in 1987, Ronald Reagan took responsibility for the Iran-Contra scandal, during which kidnappers in Iran agreed to release US hostages in exchange for weapons sold to Iran, which then went on to fund anti-Communist rebels in Nicaragua. Reagan said, "A few months ago I told the American people I did not trade arms for hostages. My heart and my best intentions still tell me that's true, but the facts and the evidence tell me it is not."

Harry S. Truman was known for keeping a sign on his desk that read, "The buck stops here." Carter borrowed the sign during his administration, and several other leaders, from Boris Johnson to Joe Biden, have quoted the sentiment when accepting responsibility for their political actions.

Even Richard Nixon, best known for his cover-up of the Watergate scandal, ultimately said, "I regret deeply any injuries that may have been done in the course of the events that led to this decision." (Though, of course, one has to wonder just how sorry he actually was considering how hard he worked to conceal his involvement, but we'll take him at his word.)

This eventually led to Bill Clinton saying, in his eulogy at Nixon's funeral in 1994, "Let the days of judging Richard Nixon on anything other than the totality of his life and career be ended."

These examples all show the potential power of a well-timed apology, but is apologizing always the best plan?

TO APOLOGIZE OR NOT TO APOLOGIZE, *THAT* IS THE QUESTION

In the past, the only thing for public figures to do was own up to their mistakes and apologize for them, or deny them completely—think, "I am not a crook," "I did not have sexual relations with that woman," and, "I didn't inhale."

There's a time to admit guilt and a time to deny—or at least spin or deflect. But in recent years, mostly due to the tribalization of America (which we'll discuss later in this chapter), apologizing is no longer the only option. In today's world, you have another choice: doubling down.

When you've made a stupid mistake, done something criminal, or behaved morally or ethically wrong, then you need to own up to it and apologize for it. But if it's something that only certain members of society have now deemed wrong or unacceptable for one reason or another—essentially, if you've become the latest victim of cancel culture—you don't always have to apologize.

People are getting canceled for things they don't necessarily think are wrong—or not wrong enough to warrant the repercussions they're forced to suffer. A perfect example of this is Al Franken, the former senator from Minnesota. He was a comedian prior to entering politics, and on comedy tours years ago he made some inappropriate advances toward women that he thought were in jest. He apologized but was ultimately forced to resign his position in 2018. Looking back on his story now, he probably didn't need to go as far as he did. He likely could have apologized and moved on—and saved his Senate career in the process.

The opposite example—of someone who did own up to a mistake and was then determined to move on—is Ralph Northam, the governor of Virginia from 2018 to 2022.

In 2019, a picture from his med school yearbook was published, depicting a person in blackface and another person wearing a Ku Klux Klan hood. In the immediate aftermath, Northam issued an apology, though he later said that he didn't believe he was actually in the picture and had decided to take the blame because he was under so much pressure to respond.

After both the Democratic and Republican parties of Virginia called on him to resign, Northam held a press conference and denied being in the picture (though he admitted appearing in blackface as part of a Michael Jackson costume around the same time). Even after an investigation, it could not be conclusively determined whether he was in the photo. Northam refused to resign and remained in office, and although his approval rating initially fell to 40 percent, it rose significantly by the end of his term, during which he made a commitment to addressing Virginia's racial inequities.

Governor Northam weathered this storm, and it's now long forgotten. Why? Well, it's one thing if someone posts something offensive or poorly worded on Twitter tomorrow, and it comes back to bite them in the ass; it's quite another thing when someone intentionally trolling for dirt digs up something from more than two decades ago. We're all different people now than we were twenty years ago. But we see this all the time! Anything in your past can be dug up and used to create an instant firestorm. Fortunately, the answer is easy. If you know it was wrong, you say, "Hey, I was a child; I made immature decisions. That does not reflect who I am today."

"But, Wesley," you may be thinking, "maybe they won't find out! Maybe I can just *hide* whatever I would have to apologize for if it were to be made public."

In the age of the internet, anything you've done, anything you've said, or the person you are in the shadows will always be brought to light. There's no hiding. We have all the world's information at the tips of our fingers. I can Google anything about anyone anywhere and figure out who they are, what they believe, and what they've done. So don't try to hide it. It's better to just get it out, be honest and authentic, apologize, and let the news cycle move on.

WHETHER YOU DO OR DON'T
APOLOGIZE, BE AUTHENTIC

In the past five to ten years, there's been a lot of rethinking about whether to apologize even if you don't believe you've done anything wrong. The rule of thumb I'd like to put forward is to *be authentic*. If you're truly sorry, say so! People will identify with that authenticity. If you're not sorry—if you feel justified in your actions and don't believe you did anything wrong—you need to be authentic and say just that. Again, people will identify with your authenticity, whichever way you go.

> Whether you are apologizing or doubling down, you have to own it. Sometimes you're owning the fact that you are wrong; other times, you're owning that you're *not* wrong. Either way, you have to take a hard stance.

When you are authentic, your apology is most likely going to land correctly. But if it comes across as inauthentic, that's when you get in trouble. If you apologize and people think you don't mean it, you're actually going to hurt yourself more. Similarly, if you double down and back up the things you did, but people can see that you actually regret it, you'll also take a hit. Authenticity is always the answer when it comes to responding to these kinds of crises.

If you just act like a decent human being, that will get you most of the way there, and you'll gain the empathy of your audience. Hell, we've all screwed up and done something we shouldn't have. Everybody's been in that same spot at different times. And we want to champion someone who is seeking redemption. We want to have the opportunity to forgive people; it's human nature.

In general, being authentic doesn't take a PR expert; it's just you being human and saying you're sorry because it's the right thing to do—or defending your decision if you think you are in the right.

There's a saying in politics that candidates are either Jimmy Stewart or John Wayne. Think about these two archetypes: Jimmy Stewart represents the self-effacing everyman, someone who is able to connect with people at their level, whereas John Wayne is the hero, the epitome of toughness and swagger, looking to save you from something. Jimmy Stewart apologizes when he's caused harm; John Wayne gets angry about the injustice.

Barack Obama, Bill Clinton, and George H. W. Bush are Jimmy Stewart types; Donald Trump, Ronald Reagan, and George W. Bush are John Waynes.

> Jimmy Stewart and John Wayne are different actors who played very different roles, and people liked them for different reasons! But if John Wayne suddenly played a Jimmy Stewart character, it would come off weird (and vice versa). Similarly, when a candidate steps out of their archetype and tries to apologize like the other, it almost always comes off as inauthentic.

Being authentic also allows you to appeal to your base, and when you're caught up in a cancel-culture crisis, it is extremely important to have that base. You need to find a swath of the population that sees your point and is with you; otherwise, you're in trouble. You're done if no one's standing with you. But as long as you have that pool of support to draw from, these things are survivable—especially if you're authentic and have a good story to tell.

That's not the case, however, with someone where all the evidence is stacked against them, and public support has waned and then fled. And there's no insurance policy against this. Just look at Bill Cosby—he had a ton of goodwill. He was a beloved actor and TV host. But once he was accused of drugging and/or sexually assaulting sixty women, the evidence was overwhelming, and he lost all public opinion.

The body of an individual's work does make a difference when judging their past comments or deeds, because people look at them in totality. The Northam story I mentioned earlier in the chapter is interesting because governors are only in office for four years in Virginia, so they're relatively new and unknown in that scene. When the first thing you hear about a guy is that he did blackface, it takes up a lot of the chunk of common knowledge about that individual. Compare that to someone like Martin Luther King Jr., whose body of work and impact on society comprises the majority of most people's knowledge of him. When that's the case, people are not as focused on the negatives, so they don't mean as much in comparison.

This is also why we see TikTok and YouTube influencers get canceled on a weekly basis. They're trivial in the grand scheme of things, so they're disposable. If you are disposable and then you have something negative pop up from your past, people will automatically write you off because they don't know anything else about you.

That's also key: not only do people care about authenticity when reacting to these events, but you also have to engender some empathy on your behalf, or when you fall, you're not going to get anybody to join your side. Maintaining a sympathetic attitude with a framework of empathetic support is important.

Just think about Olympic swimmer Michael Phelps. In 2009, he was photographed holding a marijuana pipe to his mouth, leading to a three-month suspension. He had a lot of goodwill, so people were willing to write off the mistake. This is not comparable to the Bill Cosby case because, with Phelps, a lot of people thought, "Oh, it's just weed." They don't think that about rape. His apology was simple and swift, and people felt empathetic. They've been young and made stupid decisions, too; many people have smoked weed before. They think, "Hey, in the scope of life, this isn't a big deal. You're a national treasure!"

ADMIT/ACKNOWLEDGE YOUR MISTAKE, APOLOGIZE, AND MOVE ON…

So how do you apologize in a way that will help people move on quickly?

Well, if you did the crime, say you're sorry, and—as we've already covered—be authentic. That's the only way that people will respond positively to your scenario. You don't want it to linger on your conscience any longer, and it wouldn't be authentic to keep going with the way you may have been addressing the topic. I know I used Richard Nixon as an example of a politician apologizing, but if he had come out earlier and admitted, "This was done on my watch, and I take ownership," (or, hell, if he had borrowed the "buck stops here" sign), it would have prevented him from continuing to exacerbate the crisis.

There's an important distinction to be made between actually having harmed somebody and that person being overly sensitive. You should apologize if you hurt someone, but you don't need to apologize for the sensitivity of others. In today's world, people find every reason to be offended by *everything*. You can't apologize just because someone else is offended by your words, or you'll do nothing but apologize all day! You would never be able to speak out. But if you've actually hurt someone or done something to hurt a group of people, you absolutely should say you're sorry.

Your apology will be different from someone else's because your situation is different from theirs. But the one general rule all apologies should follow is that your apology should be authentic to you. The recipient or audience for that apology should believe that it actually came from you. As long as you're genuinely sorry and that authenticity comes through in your apology, it doesn't have to be complicated. It doesn't even have to be well thought out. (Unless there's a legal issue, in which case you'll want to be careful about what you admit to.)

Again, if your apology is *not* genuine, then you shouldn't apologize at all, because it's only going to do more damage. We'll talk more about this in the next section, but Donald Trump *never* apologizes. But think about it: an apology from Donald Trump wouldn't be authentic. It wouldn't fit his brand, and it absolutely would not land with his audience. So, because he's not actually sorry, there's no use in apologizing.

If it's not authentic or not really an apology, you've already lost. Again, it's better to not say sorry if that's not how you feel.

Similarly, you don't want to give a nonapology. For example, we talked in the previous chapter about Alec Baldwin's gun misfiring on the set of *Rust*. After that happened (quite a while after that happened, actually—his first misstep), he said, "I'm sorry that the woman died, but I didn't pull the trigger." That's not an apology; that's covering his ass! Saying things like, "Oh, I'm sorry your feelings got hurt," or "I'm sorry that happened," is different from saying, "I did this, and I'm sorry."

To apologize authentically, think about the recipient of the apology—both the victim of whatever happened, to whom you are directly apologizing, and the larger audience who will be observing that apology.

In a crisis scenario, it's important that the victim hears your apology, because the last thing you want is additional backlash from them saying that you don't get it, you didn't really apologize, or that you don't even know why you're sorry. That's a disaster, and we see this happen all the time in the public eye, where someone makes their attempt at an apology, and the aggrieved party comes back and dismisses the apology as worthless. You want the aggrieved party to think, "They did that. they apologized. I appreciate it." That's the best-case scenario.

The second part of the audience is everybody else who's rubbernecking, watching this disaster go down. We're all commentators on social media, becoming judges and juries of these events. This audience could say, "This guy's a jerk, he didn't mean that apology." Both the victim and the audience need to be satisfied with your apology because they both have the ability to shape the narrative.

An apology can be very simple. You have to come across as sincere, and you have to say specifically what you did that was wrong or what you did to hurt someone else and what you're going to do to rectify the problem.

Think of the parable of the Prodigal Son from the Bible. A father has two sons. One of them stays with his father, working on his farm, loyal and obedient. The other son, however, takes the money his father has promised him and leaves home, quickly "squander[ing] his wealth in wild living." Starving, he returns home to his father, where he says, "Father, I have sinned against heaven and before you; I am no longer worthy to be called your son; treat me as one of your hired servants."

Rather than being mad that his son wasted his money, the father says, "Bring quickly the best robe, and put it on him; and put a ring on his hand, and shoes on his feet; and bring the fatted calf and kill it, and let us eat and make merry; for this my son was

dead, and is alive again; he was lost, and is found."
Your apology doesn't have to be as extreme as the prodigal
son's, but asking for forgiveness is the best way to receive it.

...OR DOUBLE DOWN AND DENY WRONGDOING

So now you know what to do if you *are* sorry, but what if
you're *not*?

If you're not sorry, the only thing to do is double down and
push harder. It would be inauthentic to apologize if you don't
actually feel sorry for whatever you're being accused of, and it
won't come off well because people will see right through it. So
don't!

> It is possible to have done the crime and not be sorry
> for it. Donald Trump is a prime example of this. He
> wrote the book on doubling down and not apologizing.

We've come to this point in our culture where everybody
demands an apology for everything. No matter what you say,
you're told, "You should apologize for that." Well, now an apology doesn't mean anything anymore. If everybody's apologizing
for everything, nobody's *actually* apologizing for anything, and
apologies just don't matter.

So now, unlike in the past, you have the ability to double down.

If you're not sorry, if you feel like you're the aggrieved one, or if you have nothing to be ashamed of in the interaction, it's okay to double down and say, "You know what? Here's why I'm right and the other person's wrong."

Now, if you do this, be prepared to divide the audience. This is not a scenario where you can come out with everyone agreeing with you, and that's fine. A lot of people may not agree with you, but many others will, and those people will have your back. Be prepared to have half the audience on your side, turning it into a model he-said-she-said scenario.

Everyone has personal biases. The other side has an agenda, and that is to double down on showing why they are the victim and what's behind their accusations against you. You just have to find and display those biases. Why is the accuser saying the things they're saying? Well, it's because *they* are actually the piece of shit here.

I have to acknowledge that Donald Trump tends to do this naturally. If Nancy Pelosi calls him a jerk, he doesn't deny it; he turns it back on her: "Of course she's saying that about me. Of course they hate me! Look at what *they're* doing."

Even if he were inclined to apologize, it wouldn't land with anyone! The Democrats wouldn't believe him because it's not authentic, and his Republican followers would see that as a sign of weakness. By doubling down, he actually *strengthens* his position with his own base. Additionally, if he were to apologize for something that all his supporters do or believe, that would mean that they were in the wrong, too. His supporters don't want him to apologize because they don't want to apologize for something they believe. That's why Donald Trump does it. (I guess we can say that, at least, he is always true to himself!)

When you double down, you have to offer more than what you originally came with. Not only do you agree with what you did, but you can back it up with facts, proof, or examples. Have your team do research on all the reasons that can support your claims of why you're right—or why your accuser is actually wrong. Oftentimes, this is as simple as going back and looking at the agendas and social media posts of the person who accused you and clouding the vision they're trying to project.

Again, this will divide your audience, but it keeps you from apologizing or admitting any wrongdoing, and it puts the onus back on the other person.

Let's say you're a small business owner who got put in the spotlight in a local news segment over something stupid. You can come out and say, "I'm a business owner, and I run my business the way I want to run my business. That customer was a jerk, and they should never show their face in this establishment ever again!"

There's a certain segment of the population that, after hearing that, will think, "You know what? This guy's right. He sticks to his guns. I like him!"

You may lose some other people, but they likely weren't your strongest supporters anyway. And anyone who wants everyone to love them is setting themselves up for failure...and for no one to love them. Not just "not everybody" but "nobody." Many of the politicians I work with want 100 percent of the accolades, 100 percent of the vote. But that's an impossible proposition! If you try to please 100 percent of the population, you're going to put off so many people and end up with nobody.

When determining whether to apologize or double down, consider what will appeal most to the people who matter, the people who will support you.

When thinking through your best-of-all-worlds / worst-of-all-worlds scenarios (from Chapter 7), sometimes the best possible outcome is "My people still love me." Other times, it may be "I come out squeaky clean." Either way, thinking about your end goal will lead your decision-making process to whether you should make an apology or double down.

If you discover that something is really hot right now—it's super divisive and not gaining you any points—your best-case scenario may be to make the story go away by lowering the temperature. Well, a great way of lowering the temperature is to come out and apologize authentically immediately. There's never been one time in any back-and-forth with my wife when I've said, "I'm so sorry," that it hasn't lowered the temperature immediately. It's a great way of keeping things from boiling over.

But that might not be your end goal. Your goal might be "I need to bloody the other side because they're relentless. It doesn't matter how much we admit wrong or apologize, they're never going to stop." In that case, you might want to double down.

In most scenarios where you're doubling down, you may have made the assumption that you've already lost. Even the term "double down" comes from gambling; it's a risk proposition. You've already lost. All your outs are gone, so you're going to double down in hopes that you hit a blackjack.

Well, it's the same thing in public relations and crisis communications. You're doubling down because you're already kind of screwed. You're looking to salvage what's left of your winnings and go home with at least some of the audience who loves and trusts you.

Examples of Doubling Down, for Better or Worse

Gina Carano is a good example of someone who didn't fare so well but didn't apologize, either. She's a former mixed martial artist who became an actress on the Star Wars TV show *The Mandalorian*. After posting on social media that the 2020 presidential election was based on voter fraud, making fun of people wearing masks during the COVID-19 pandemic, and comparing "hating someone for their political views" to the Holocaust, Lucasfilm and her talent agency dropped her. She lost her job on one of the biggest shows in the world, but she didn't apologize for it. She never backed down from her position because she thought she was morally right. And because of that, she's become something of a conservative star (though a pariah on Disney+).

Then you have Kevin Spacey. In 2017, an actor accused Spacey of making sexual advances against him. He denied it, claiming not to remember the events and even coming out as gay in an attempt to change the conversation, but fifteen more people came forward to accuse him of sexual abuse. The evidence against him was overwhelming, in the court of public opinion, if not in a court of law, and ultimately his career tanked.

Finally, think about Brett Kavanaugh. Despite allegations of sexual assault against him, he's never apologized, he's continued to double down on his innocence, and he's now a Supreme Court Justice.

SEAWORLD SAYS, "I'M SORRY"

Even large corporations have to say, "I'm sorry," sometimes.

That became one of our strategies when working with SeaWorld to rehab their image after PETA's attacks. They admitted some fault and said, "You know what? We hear you. It's time to stop breeding orcas in captivity."

Their CEO went on *Good Morning America* and *The Today Show* in a massive media blitz to talk about SeaWorld's decision to stop their breeding program, highlighting that the current generation of killer whales will be the last ones born in captivity.

And that apology was exactly what SeaWorld's supporters wanted to hear. Attendance at the parks increased after the announcement, and brand favorability increased 7 percent in the first quarter of 2018—its first improvement in sentiment in years.

Whether you follow in SeaWorld's footsteps and apologize or do like the Donald and double down, make the best choice for yourself and your supporters. You'll need them on your side as we move into Chapter 9, because if they're not with you they're against you. It's time to get clear on who your enemies are.

KNOW AND LABEL YOUR OPPONENT

**"If you know the enemy and know yourself, you
need not fear the result of a hundred battles.
If you know yourself but not the enemy, for
every victory gained you will also suffer a
defeat. If you know neither the enemy nor
yourself, you will succumb in every battle."
—Sun Tzu, *The Art of War***

After the end of World War II, General George S. Patton said
that America "defeated the wrong enemy."

Patton meant that, although the US obviously had good
reason to fight in Germany, they weren't the *real* enemy;

the Soviet Union and Communism were. If we fast-forward through history a bit, we know that after the Soviet Union collapsed, it became Russia. As I write this, in 2022, Russia is invading Ukraine, proving that, at least in some part, General Patton was right.

Additionally, when Mitt Romney was running for president, he was asked, "Who's the biggest problem America faces?" He answered, "Russia," and everybody made fun of him, saying things like, "Man, is he out of touch. He's stuck in the Cold War! He doesn't know what he's talking about."

Today we see that those people were wrong, and that Patton and Romney nailed it. They read the signs and knew who the greatest threat to freedom would be.

They knew their opponent.

MAKE SURE YOU'RE FIGHTING THE RIGHT ENEMY

We live in a very divisive world, one that has been trending more in this direction for a while. There are always two sides to every story and two teams in every crisis. To make it clear who is on your side, you have to make it clear who is *not* on your side; you have to label the opposition.

This is in the context of when you are wrongly attacked—not if you're the perpetrator, as we saw in the last chapter, but when something is perpetrated against you. When this occurs, it's important to identify who's perpetrating these rumors or scandals upon you and expose their ulterior motives.

Everyone consuming the scandal has been wronged by someone else. Because this is such a common phenomenon, there's a natural feeling of empathy toward the individual having a scandal foisted upon them, as long as the other side looks less sympathetic. In the world of public opinion, you want to make sure the other side's bias is known to the people consuming the information. "They're saying I'm the bad guy, but they're coming after me because I'm actually the good guy, and *they* are the bad ones!" This is what Donald Trump does so beautifully.

A lot of times you can win a battle through division. When you can define your enemy, you also label your allies. The intention is to create an us-versus-them mentality, to draw a line in the sand and say, "Choose a side." Then you recruit those allies to have your back. "These people who are against me are the same people who are against you."

> This is how Donald Trump was elected. Nobody voted for Donald Trump because he stood for anything; he had enemies that his voters hated, and he called out his enemies as the bad guys.

Representative Alexandria Ocasio-Cortez, for example, is very popular with her base. The hardcore conservatives who don't like what she's saying are the people who come after her. So, for the base that she endears herself to, the context under which she's being attacked is a false one. None of those attacks are ever going to stick; she's survived those attacks, and she'll continue to survive.

When you have a far-left candidate like her, the only effective attacks would have to come from the left. If AOC gets attacked from someone on the left, it knocks the base out from under her and causes her to come off balance because she's created a platform by which she is the arbiter of all things left. But if all of a sudden she's not representative of the leftist way, then the authenticity of her arguments fall on bad ground. When she is attacked from the right, however, the context is there. Of course you don't like her; she's the hero of the left.

When you are in crisis, you can say, "These people or groups are coming after me," which then enables you to rally your supporters around your cause. But before you can know who may be an ally, you have to first know who your enemy is.

FIRST, FIGURE OUT WHO'S THE BADDIE

The first step is to identify your enemy. This is important because, in the fog of war that comes in the middle of a cancel-culture crisis, you may misidentify where the attacks are actually coming from.

The enemy in crisis communications is often labeled as the press because they're the ones covering the story and asking the tough questions. But, more often than not, there's someone else behind their inquisition, someone pushing a story. The press is not the real enemy; they just become the tactical conduit through which the crisis has taken shape. But who is? Who's the person instigating these questions from the press?

While I was writing this book, a client called me because the press had just left a message on his phone saying that a staffer had seen something pornographic in his browser history and tipped off the reporter.

Who's the enemy here? It's not the reporter, who is just doing their job; it's whoever decided to pitch the story to the press—and whoever may be behind that person, guiding their actions. In this case, we'll have to figure out who the enemy really is, but it's pretty obvious that it's one of his opponents.

There is typically a fairly obvious opponent for a politician, but similarly, the enemy can be pretty obvious for a small business owner or the average person as well. I can't tell you specifically who your enemy may be, but you should have a pretty good idea if you take a look at your competition or detractors.

Additionally, if you've been a small business owner since 2020, you're going to realize that one of your enemies may be your local council or state legislators. Since the beginning of the COVID-19 pandemic, most businesses have been absolutely crushed by regulations. You could say the enemy is COVID-19, but in practical terms, it's the people who are saying, "Your business can't be open right now," or "You can only operate at 50 percent capacity." That's the crisis most people have been dealing with. I own a brewery, and we had to completely shut down for three months. Once we were able to reopen, we had to operate at or below 50 percent capacity.

So you have to ask yourself where the questions or attacks are coming from. It could be a former employee or a disgruntled customer. Who's fueling this? Who stands to benefit from your crisis? *That's* the actual enemy.

Figuring out where the attack is *really* coming from is important so you don't aim your fire at someone who is just doing their job. You often see this in local news stories, when a business owner starts to get belligerent with the reporter interviewing them. This is a fairly commonplace scenario, but that's the wrong target! You don't want to just piss into the wind, because that *will* blow back on you. If you aim your fire at the wrong person, you're going to look like a jerk.

SOMETIMES *YOU* ARE YOUR OWN WORST ENEMY

The previous examples are all external enemies, but enemies can be internal as well. In this day and age of cancel culture run amok, many times an individual creates their own problems. This was not always the case for traditional crises, but in today's cancel-culture world, the majority of these wounds are self-inflicted. (Approximately 90 percent of my podcast *Under Fire* is talking about exactly that: people who cause their own problems.)

A good example (which we talked about in the previous chapter) is Alec Baldwin and the gun going off on the set of *Rust*. He was the producer of that movie. He was the person in charge of the set. He was the person *holding* the gun. His response to the situation was horrible, and that's all on him, nobody else.

Similarly, the anti-worker movement on Reddit is, for the most part, about bosses being pieces of shit and letting their egos rage out of control. There are a few people on there who are being too sensitive, but many people are rightly calling out bosses who treat their employees like garbage and who are causing their own problems.[4]

So how can you identify if you might be getting in your own way? Answer the following questions as honestly as possible:

- Are your own words the controversy?
- Do you spend hours each day on social media? If so, are you addicted to social media?
- Do you troll people on social media?

---

4   Here's another example of a CEO shooting themselves in the foot: https://thehustle.co/gerald-ratners-billion-dollar-speech/

- Do you have a hard time controlling yourself when drinking or doing drugs?
- Do you have a hard time controlling your sexual urges?
- Do you have a hard time telling the truth?
- Are you constantly getting in the way of your own success?

If you answered yes to any of these questions, you are probably your own worst enemy.

> More often than not, people are canceled for their own actions; it's not because someone else is coming after them. You have to confront the fact that the cause of your crisis might not be somebody throwing you under the bus. You might be painting the target on your own back.

NEXT, IDENTIFY YOUR ENEMY'S MOTIVES

Once you've identified your enemy, the next step is to identify their motives. Again, we'll look at both internal and external enemies.

You Have Your Reasons

If you discover that your enemy is yourself, you're probably not causing yourself harm on purpose. It's likely a joke, something being taken out of context, or failing to think something through before speaking or posting on social media.

Ask yourself, "What were my motives? Why did I do or say what I did?"

The reason this gets people in trouble is because there is no winning. Once you've defined the goal as wanting to get this story to end, continuing to try to prove yourself works directly against that goal. It continues the story.

If you've identified that you are getting in your own way, it's time for some self-assessment. Why are you drinking like that? Why do you feel the need to keep responding? I can't answer that for you. Go to a counselor if you feel like you have a larger problem. Figure out why the hell you're acting like that.

Each and every one of us has a fundamental flaw inside of us, so we all have to perform some self-actualization to figure out why we act in ways that are contrary to our best interests. As Socrates said, "To know thyself is the beginning of wisdom."

But if you are your own worst enemy, know that you're not alone. This even happened to me. (I know!) I was canceled for a tweet, which eventually led to Keith Olbermann naming me the "worst person in the world" on MSNBC. (In the *world*! Quite an honor.)

We were talking about a voter ID issue, and someone tweeted about Black college students voting in multiple states. I responded, "This is why we need voter ID." I *meant* that we needed it so people weren't able to vote twice, but people took it to mean that I was against Black students voting. It went viral, and the national news picked it up. I thought I was being funny, but no one else did, and all hell broke loose.

This was just as I described: a self-inflicted wound caused by trying to be funny on Twitter, not thinking things through, and saying something stupid. Additionally, once I examined my motives, I realized that I always wanted to prove myself. I always wanted to win the fight. That was my motivation, and that got me into trouble.

I thought I was joking, but it was taken out of context because there's no nuance online. No one will ever give you the benefit of the doubt and assume you're joking; they will take your words at face value—or twist them into something way worse—and they will come after you.

I obviously should have known better, but I let my ego get the best of me—just as other people do every single day. Today I would know not to touch the topic at all; it's not worth it. The cons far outweigh any potential benefits that could come of it, and there's no way to think about all the different ways someone can twist the meaning of your words.

If you're a professional at all (and you likely are because you're reading this book), know this: none of these social media fights are worth it. None of them. Don't be your own worst enemy, running into a field of land mines. You might get through that field, but you might get your leg blown off in the process. It's just not worth the risk.

They Have Their Reasons, Too

The worst thing you can do in a crisis scenario is have the story be all about you. You must label and name the enemy because you want the other side to be a part of the story. Once you know *who* they are, the next thing to consider is *why* they're doing this. Why are they saying this about you? You have to specifically say, "These are the people coming after me, and *here's why*."

In doing so, you are contextualizing the scenario and allowing people to take a side. If the allegations against you are all the information people have, then they're *going* to be against you. But when you show them who the other side is and why they might be attacking you, you can bring people to your side.

To do that, you have to label your enemies and their motivations, and you have to be clear about it. Keep it simple. I had a mentor who said, "If you can say it in three sentences, say three sentences, but if you can make it two, that's even better, and one sentence is better than two."

The less you say—and the more direct, straightforward, and clear you are—the less your words can be used against you, and the greater the salience of the attack you're making.

- "X person or group is attacking me because they don't like that I do Y."
- "Democrats are attacking me because I want to build the border wall."

The motivation for whoever revealed that my client may have looked at porn online is to make him look bad, especially in the eyes of people for whom that would be shocking. His primary voters are right-wing Christian conservatives who will think, "He looks at porn; that's not family values."

Everybody has a selfish motive these days. They're using your mistake, your words, for some political advantage.

As another example, on the Friday before Memorial Day of 2021, Kamala Harris tweeted a picture of herself and said, "Enjoy the long weekend." Conservatives pounced on her for allegedly not respecting our fallen heroes! She didn't actually hurt or offend anybody, but they needed *something* to come after her for, and she gave them the handbook to attack the liberals and say, "Look, they're anti-American! They don't love America as much as we do."

But that backfires too: if you're so caught up with attacking Kamala Harris on Memorial Day, then maybe you don't care all that much about Memorial Day, either. It's not like those conservatives were sitting at home mourning the dead from Friday until Tuesday morning. They were out drinking and grilling and buying mattresses on sale just like everybody else.

Look for the selfish reason. You know who your enemies are. What is their self-serving reason for coming after you right now?

FINALLY, IDENTIFY YOUR ENEMY'S NEXT MOVE

Once you know who your enemy is and their motivation, you can start to predict their strategies and tactics. Just like chess, you have to know where they're going to move before you can plan the best move to make for yourself. If you don't know who's making the move, you can't predict what the next hit is going to be. When you *do* know this, however, you can prepare for any hits that may be coming or go on the offensive yourself.

Different classes of enemies are going to have different strategies available to them. The average angry consumer or former employee is only going to have so much leverage they can use. If the crisis is not self-inflicted, a businessperson is going to face attacks that come from either a competing business down the road or legislation that is restricting their business's operations.

Once we get into political or public relations battles, the field gets a lot wider. If you're talking about a US Senate candidate, the enemy could be the opposition, it could be a super PAC, or it could be the opposing national party.

But whoever the enemy is, and wherever those attacks are coming from, how can you predict their strategies, and what should your moves be as a result?

There are two things you can do. First, put yourself in the shoes of the opposition. If you were on their side of the table and you did X, what would their next move be? Then jump back to your side of the table and analyze how you would respond if they made that move.

Second, in addition to trying to put yourself in their strategic position, you can also analyze your enemy's personal characteristics. Are they calm, or are they hotheaded? Think of yourself as a boxer. A boxer knows if the person they're fighting tends to swing left first.

Not only do you have to put yourself in your opponent's position; you also have to put yourself in *their specific brain.* Analyze your opponent. Know how they typically move. When you know who the opposition is at that level, you'll know what they're going to do with what you give them, so you can predict even *more* moves ahead.

Whether it's political campaigns, crisis communications, or cancel culture, all public relations is about projecting the actions of others into scenarios that may or may not come to pass. Think of Littlefinger in *Game of Thrones.* He's a schemer, and he says something that applies perfectly here:

> Don't fight in the North or the South. Fight every battle, every-where, always, in your mind. Everyone is your enemy, everyone is your friend. Every possible series of events is happening all at

once. Live that way and nothing will surprise you. Everything that happens will be something that you've seen before.

When you have a mental schema for all the possible scenarios that could happen, you're able to react in a calm and measured way when one inevitably does without making missteps or falling into a trap.

When you have some idea of what to expect, you also have a better idea of what to prepare for. The reverse is also true. You're going to find yourself continually stepping in it if you don't anticipate your opponent's response.

Bruce Lee said, "Be like water making its way through cracks. Do not be assertive, but adjust to the object, and you shall find a way around or through it. If nothing within you stays rigid, outward things will disclose themselves. Empty your mind, be formless. Shapeless, like water. If you put water into a cup, it becomes the cup. You put water into a bottle and it becomes the bottle. You put it in a teapot, it becomes the teapot. Now, water can flow or it can crash. Be water, my friend."[5]

He was talking about fighting his enemy, and he knew what he was talking about. If you're too rigid and haven't thought through what your enemy's move is going to be, then you're

---

5   Bruce Lee and John Little, *Bruce Lee's Striking Thoughts*, (Tokyo: Tuttle Publishing, 2002).

going to get hit. But if you're like water—if you move *with* their move—you're able to react faster.

I want to share one last quote with you to round out this section, and it comes again from General Patton: "A battle is already won or lost before armies ever take the battlefield."

Generals are always in the background thinking about the moves both sides must make in order for one to win. You are in the same situation. It's like Schrödinger's public relations: until you make a comment, you are both dead and alive; the battle is both won and lost.

By identifying your enemy's strategies, you can both learn how to protect yourself, *and* you can get off the defensive and potentially go on the offensive. First, you block their punch, and then you take it back to them. The best defense is offense, after all, and you can't just sit back and let the attacks keep coming. Once you know who to attack, however—and what their next move may be—then your offensive strategy can become clearer as well.

KNOW THINE ENEMY

SeaWorld had to follow these same principles before we could determine the best strategy for them.

First, they had to know who their enemy was and *wasn't*. Sure, the average person may have watched *Blackfish* or even decided they didn't like SeaWorld anymore, but they were not the enemy.

The normal, everyday public were the people SeaWorld wanted at its parks. So who was driving them away with all these attacks?

A bunch of random people rarely coalesce to attack a formerly beloved institution; there's almost always an organizing force. Who was the force behind *Blackfish*? PETA. Enemy identified.

Next, what were PETA's motives?

Well, it helps to know that PETA had already single-handedly shut down Barnum & Bailey. That effort had generated the majority of PETA's funding, so once they accomplished that mission, they looked around for a new target, and that's when they set their sights on SeaWorld. PETA was able to fundraise and make tens of millions of dollars by attacking them and generating hate against them.

Based on PETA's previous actions, we could start predicting what else they might throw into the battlefield. That's what allowed us to stop playing only defense and switch to offense. We went after PETA hard, launching an effort to inform the public that PETA actually owns the largest kill mills in America, putting more animals to sleep than any other group in the country.

Recognizing that PETA was behind the attack and labeling them as the enemy also helped when it came to recruiting allies. PETA are a bunch of left-wing liberal nutjobs, so we could say, "Hey, conservatives, these are your enemies, too. We're fighting the same enemy, so you need to have our back."

After all, "The enemy of my enemy is my friend." We could show that these weren't normal people coming after us; they were the absolute nutjob wackos who had covered themselves in blood and sat in meat trays outside of the US Capitol. They're nuts!

We were able to rally all these conservatives around us because we had a common enemy in PETA.

There was just one opportunity we missed in our fight, and it's one you're going to learn about next. If you want to win *fast*, you have to be the one to get the facts out *first*.

CHAPTER 10

GET ALL THE FACTS
OUT *BEFORE* THEY DO

"The time is coming when everything that is
covered up will be revealed, and all that is secret
will be made known to all. Whatever you have
said in the dark will be heard in the light, and
what you have whispered behind closed doors will
be shouted from the housetops for all to hear."
—Luke 12:2–3, New Living Translation

ave you seen the 2002 movie *8 Mile*? In it, Eminem plays
a semi-autobiographical, up-and-coming rapper in Detroit.
He chokes in the initial rap battle, during which two rap-
pers deliver personal attacks on each other, even vomiting

on himself ("Mom's spaghetti"). At the very end of the movie, though, Eminem's character B-Rabbit is going up against Papa Doc (played by Anthony Mackie). Papa Doc wins the coin toss to determine their order, and he says, "Let that bitch go first." (Big mistake!)

Instead of starting by attacking Papa Doc, B-Rabbit lists everything Papa Doc could potentially say about him: basically, that he's white trash who lives in a trailer park with his mom, that his friends do stupid shit, that Papa Doc's gang beat him up, and that one of B-Rabbit's former friends hooked up with his girlfriend.

By the time Papa Doc (whose real name, we have devastatingly learned, is Clarence) comes up to the mic, he has nothing left to say. In a satisfying reversal from the beginning of the movie, it is the villain's turn to choke because Eminem had already used up all of the ammo that could potentially be used against him.

DON'T LET YOUR OPPONENT, OR THE
MEDIA, CONTROL THE NARRATIVE

You, too, can use what I call the Eminem strategy by *taking control of the narrative.*

If you get out all the information about yourself before your enemies can, they don't have anything to use to attack you. Part of why Donald Trump was able to weather so much is because people already know the worst things about him. He's been famous for thirty years. We already know he's had business failures, had personal drama, and supported liberal causes (including Hillary Clinton). You can't really attack him on any of those things, because they're all common knowledge.

If you have vulnerabilities—and we all do—you need to be the arbiter of how those vulnerabilities are exposed and fleshed out in the media narrative. You can do it or your opponent can do it, but your opponents will not be as gracious with those facts as you will. Get those facts out and spin them the way you need to. This is a crisis; the very last thing you need is death by a thousand cuts. Get it all out at once and then focus on stopping the bleeding.

Bill Clinton's scandal with Monica Lewinsky will be studied forever because his denial of what happened made it worse, not better. If he had said, "I did have an affair; here's what happened," it may have cauterized the bleeding rather than dragging it out for as long as it did.

This is, of course, easier said than done. It's human nature to cover up. This goes back to the Garden of Eden, when Adam and Eve hid themselves from God even though they knew it was wrong. Sometimes we do this because we're ashamed or embarrassed, like when someone is caught cheating on their spouse. Other times, we do this out of self-preservation to avoid getting hurt or going to jail.

But in crisis management, you frequently have to do things that are counterintuitive. Your first instincts are often wrong, and you'll have to do the opposite. In this case, you'll have to uncover some of what you'd rather keep hidden, but with the goal of controlling how it comes out.

I often say that when you have something to hide you can save face, or you can save your ass, but you can't save both. You can preserve your job, or you can preserve people's vision of you, but it's almost impossible to do both. You've got to pick one, and the other has to be sacrificed.

There are instances where you can say, "This happened a long time ago, here's what went down. These are all the facts, some of them may be unseemly, so make of it what you will." That strategy not only gets the facts out; it also prevents you from being blackmailed.

There are fewer examples of this scenario, partly because when you do this, there tends *not* to be a scandal. One example, though, is Pete Buttigieg, a Democratic presidential candidate and secretary of transportation. He knew he was gay growing up, and he always thought that would make it impossible to ever run for political office. It wasn't until he came out that his star began to rise—because he was forthright and honest about himself, and he wasn't going to hide who he was or open himself up to being blackmailed. Buttigieg was the mayor of South Bend, Indiana, when he came out, and to his surprise, it really bolstered his political career rather than killing it, even in a conservative state.

As we learned in the previous chapter, people love authenticity; they want you to be honest and real with them. No one's perfect, and no one expects you to be, but they *do* expect you to be honest and to own up to mistakes. Everybody has those things in their life they're ashamed of or troubles they've been through that they try to put behind them. When you're honest and real about these scenarios, it gives you a level of freedom and cover in the mind of the public that you otherwise wouldn't have.

As George Burns put it, "Sincerity is the most important thing—if you can fake that, you can do anything!"

HOW TO TAKE (BACK) CONTROL
OF THE NARRATIVE

It may not be possible to keep from ceding control of the narrative or to be the first one out there. At this point, you're already in crisis. This book is what happens once you've already stepped in the shit. Obviously, the best thing to do next time is to look where you're going so you might not step in a pile of dog shit, but that doesn't get your shoes clean *now*.

Let's take a look at what to do after that shit has already hit the fan.

Step One: Rapid Response

The first step is to respond as fast as possible.

This shouldn't be much of a surprise, as we've talked about this in other chapters (most recently, Chapter 7). You already know that SeaWorld lost control of the narrative because they didn't respond for an entire year.

Travis Scott *completely* lost control of the narrative with the whole Astroworld fiasco. First, he should have controlled the atmosphere while he was onstage. Stop singing, slow everybody down, even yell at the audience. (Dave Grohl, the lead singer of the Foo Fighters, is great at this.) Travis Scott had the opportunity to stop the bleeding before it got bad, but he didn't.

He also had the opportunity to take back control of the narrative after the concert, after people had already been trampled and were taken to the hospital, but instead, he was out partying with Kylie Jenner and Drake at Dave & Buster's (of all fucking places!). Not only did he not respond onstage, but he didn't respond immediately afterward, so the story got out of control as people kept tweeting videos, and the media picked it up.

What can you learn from his tale of woe? What should he (and his team) have done differently?

His team should have had someone come onstage to tell him what was going on so he could stop *immediately*. Failing that, as soon as he came off stage, they should have told him what the problem was and prepared a response. He could have gone to the hospital and checked on people, talked with the families, shown his concern. Imagine how different the reaction would have been if people saw him sitting there all night, showing that he cared about his fans, saying, "I'm not leaving this hospital until you do."

Step Two: Get the Facts Out Fast

The second step is to be transparent and get out all the facts as you see them.

You've already read the Mark Twain quote about how far a lie can travel before the truth gets out of bed in the morning. While that lie can travel around the world, you ideally need to stop it before it gets out of the city, state, continent, or across the ocean. That's very difficult to do in today's digital world, but it is also because of that digital world that you have the ability to respond immediately, and you can reach those same people who may have heard the first damaging message.

Once a message gets out, it's out there. But if you respond immediately, then your response can get out there just as fast as the message. If cable news is covering the situation, you want them to be able to cover *both* sides of the story, immediately. "This person was accused of X, and here's their immediate response.

They said that's bullshit, and here's the whole truth behind this. This is what's really going on."

If a crisis is breaking out, you have to be the person controlling the direction of the story. If you don't, someone else will, whether that's your enemy, the press, or just a bunch of online onlookers. You can't just let it flow out; you have to get your arms wrapped around the story. You're always going to be the best person to step forward and say what's best about you, your company, and what you do.

> Here's another question people ask me all the time: "Should I do some brand marketing?" Well, if you don't brand yourself, someone else will. And they'll never be as positive as you're going to brand yourself. The same is true for what you would say about yourself during a crisis versus what anyone else is likely to say.

A lot of times, people will say, "You shouldn't give them the benefit of responding." That's an old line of thinking. We're talking about the digital age now. You don't have a choice today because that lie can reach everybody in the world, and if you don't negate it, people will assume it's the truth. Gone are the days when you could just stay quiet and have people assume, "Oh, he's above the fray." Nope, now that's seen as a silent admission of guilt.

It's important to note that responding does not mean getting into a pissing contest with every troll who comments on social media. Public perception becomes the truth, so your response should stick to getting out the actual facts. If you don't—if you keep replying to everyone who makes a comment—that would be like if Eminem had nailed his rap battle, but then Papa Doc responded and Eminem stood onstage and replied to every single insult. He doesn't need to do this, though, because he already got the facts out there. Mic drop, boom.

CHANGE THE STORY

No matter what, you have to do something to disrupt the narrative. SeaWorld didn't get the facts out first—they let PETA get initial control of the narrative—so they had to play catch-up and get the correct information out.

After they hired us, we were able to guide them both to counterattack (as we talked about in the last chapter) and to take control of the narrative in two ways.

First, they turned the park inside out. Previously, when people went to SeaWorld, they saw dolphins jumping and roller coasters running, but behind the scenes was another story: facilities full of banged-up sea turtles and manatees with giant slashes across their bodies, all of those programs there with the sole purpose of rescuing animals and nursing them back to health. But the public couldn't see that, and it was important they did.

Back then, their thought was, "Well, we don't want someone to see a dolphin whose fin is half cut off or a beluga whale with a massive scar down its side." Our argument was, "You *absolutely* want the public to see that!"

By giving the public a transparent look at what SeaWorld did, they let everyone see that they are the world's leading rescue and rehabilitation organization for sea life. That campaign, From Park to Planet, let people know that by coming to see those animals at the park, they were also helping SeaWorld's mission of saving animals out in the wild.

We crafted their narrative and, for the first time, told their story: SeaWorld does more and spends more money to save animals across the world than any other company or government.

When two beluga whales got stuck outside of a dam here in South Carolina, SeaWorld sent boats from Florida to save those whales. When a sea lion wandered away from the California coast and onto the freeway, SeaWorld came to the rescue. But nobody was hearing those stories even though they happen all the time. SeaWorld thought that good people didn't run their mouths about what they do, following Jesus's quote of, "When you pray, do not be like the hypocrites, for they love to pray standing in the synagogues and on the street corners to be seen by men...but when you pray, go into your room, close the door and pray to your father who is unseen." They were being humble and doing good deeds in silence, so of course nobody knew this was happening!

We flipped that around and started publicizing all the rescues on social media. We pushed the public relations side of things so that every single time there was a rescue, we got it out in the press and made sure cameras were there to show SeaWorld helping that sea lion on the interstate.

The second thing SeaWorld did to change the narrative was to give PETA a small win—the end of killer whale breeding (as you learned about in the last chapter)—to shut them up. In effect, they handed PETA the microphone at the end of the rap battle and said, "What else you got?"

We starved them of a response, and you're going to learn to do that, too. In Chapter 11, you'll see why it's important not to feed the trolls.

DON'T FEED THE TROLLS

"Arguing with anonymous strangers on the Internet is a sucker's game because they almost always turn out to be—or to be indistinguishable from—self-righteous sixteen-year-olds possessing infinite amounts of free time."
—Neal Stephenson, *Cryptonomicon*

n 2018, Roseanne Barr was *back*. Her sitcom *Roseanne* had been rebooted and was receiving high ratings. And then one night, after a few drinks and an Ambien, she tweeted something crazy, saying that Valerie Jarrett, Barack Obama's former White House adviser (who is Black and was born in Iran), was like "Muslim brotherhood & planet of the apes had a baby."

The makers of Ambien went on to say, "While all pharmaceutical treatments have side effects, racism is not a known side effect of any Sanofi medication."

Although she deleted the tweet and initially apologized, as the story went viral, she responded to everybody, and her responses sounded equally as crazy as her initial remarks.

It got so bad that ABC canceled her show entirely, ultimately re-rebooting it as *The Conners*, without Roseanne anywhere near it.

The craziest thing about this is that the whole crisis took place online, mostly on Twitter. Nothing actually happened in real life. Even crazier? She likely wouldn't have gotten this response if she just had not fed the trolls.

DON'T ENGAGE THE CRAZIES ONLINE

Before I tell you not to feed the trolls, I want to make it clear what an online troll is and where they come from. (We're not talking about that toy with the hair from the nineties, and it's not some kind of monster who lives under a bridge in a fairy tale, either.)

A lot of people out there are extremely dissatisfied with their lives. They live in studio apartments in big cities or in their mom's basement in small towns and have jobs that are going nowhere. These kinds of people find value and purpose in rallying for a cause on the internet. This newer phenomenon gives them purpose in what is otherwise a fairly sad existence. And there are a lot of people on all sides of every issue doing this.

Much of cancel culture exists because America is in such a great place and everybody is so comfortable. In previous generations, people were worried about World War II, the Korean War, and the Vietnam War. Now, there are no major wars in the US, and everybody is making money.

Of course, as I was editing this book, Russia invaded Ukraine, and now we're seeing people with a similar culture to ours having to flee their homes as missiles are being dropped on their cities. But we're watching this on the news. Here in America, we're safe. We're not facing the atrocities that the people of Tel Aviv, Palestine, certain African countries, Ukraine, or Crimea are. They have real shit to be worried about: safety, shelter, and food. Yes, we have COVID, and of course, we always have homeless people, but we aren't melting snow to have drinking water or packing what we can carry and leaving our homes for the relative safety of refugee centers.

Everything is going *so* well here, in fact, that people are going online looking for these nitpicky fights because they don't really have anything else to worry about.

America is more comfortable than it's ever been in its existence and, frankly, more comfortable than any nation in history. Because everybody is so comfortable, because they have no real problems, they are looking to create them. They are searching for ways to stir up drama.

> We're going to talk more in this chapter about podcaster Joe Rogan. In the grand scheme of things, who gives a fuck what Joe Rogan says? But because people don't have anything real to worry about in their lives, it's become such a massive focal point for their ire.

Remember learning about Maslow's hierarchy of needs in school? Well, it's real. We're not really worried about shelter, clothing, or feeding ourselves anymore, and there's this fighting instinct that's been part of our DNA for ten thousand years, where we're constantly looking over our shoulders for the attacking lion. We have to have an enemy. We need an antagonist. But we don't have a lion chasing us anymore. We're not being drafted into a war. Although we're dealing with COVID-19, we have tools to fight it, so we're not really battling a horrible plague. Even in the middle of a pandemic, everybody is more or less able to continue living their lives. Two or three hundred years ago, COVID-19 would have wiped us out. We wouldn't have time to troll each other. Things have gotten easy. And so, especially in the digital realm, we're taking this need for a fight to these bizarre extremes.

> Reality TV is so popular because people are craving a fight and like watching all this drama.

Additionally, it's hard work to be an activist in real life. You have to organize, talk with people face-to-face, go knocking door to door, run for office. All of this is very tough. Becoming an "activist" online (for any side of any cause you can think of), though, is incredibly easy, and it feeds a hole in certain people's lives. Trolls like to think they're solving the world's problems by tweeting about them.

According to communication theory, in order to communicate effectively there must be a messenger and a receiver. The messenger delivers a message to the receiver, and then the receiver becomes the messenger, and the messenger becomes the receiver, going back and forth throughout the course of a conversation. Well, in internet cancel culture, there are only messengers. Everybody is speaking and no one is listening. Because of that, it doesn't matter what you say, you'll never convince anyone to change their minds.

Additionally, when everybody is talking and nobody is listening, and you try to step into that noise to defend yourself—when you respond or feed the trolls—you are participating in that feedback loop, so you also get a little hit of dopamine. But that doesn't serve you. It doesn't fill your belly. It doesn't do what you need it to do, which is to end the crisis.

So what do you have to do to get back to that place where you feel good? Well, you have to respond more. One response almost always leads to a second and a third and a fourth. You find yourself in a crazy cycle that exacerbates the trolling. Suddenly, all of your time is consumed by feeding internet trolls. This doesn't contribute to your benefit in solving this crisis; it's literally just talking to the wall.

The problem is that because they're actively looking for the fight, when you engage with those trolls—when you fight back—you're giving them exactly what they want. You are validating their existence. It creates a feedback loop that is not advantageous to you or your cause. None of that is ever going to get them to back down or to help there be fewer trolls.

So it's simple: *Don't feed the trolls.*

INSTEAD, RALLY THE TROOPS

Now, you may be thinking, "Well, if I just put out this *one* response, I'm addressing what they got wrong. If they just hear my side of the story, they'll understand!"

That is a valid point, but not necessarily in the way you may think.

It's never beneficial to feed the trolls. They're not listening, and they're never going to change their minds anyway. But what you *can* do is rally the troops.

There are people who agree with you, who see your point of view. This may sound slightly Machiavellian, but you want to validate their bias with the truth because that helps make them louder. Rather than you going up against a troll alone, these like-minded allies will engage in the battle online for you. They're speaking on your behalf. They're defending you. They're going to bat *for* you rather than you doing it on your own, and that is way more powerful than you defending yourself.

Instead of dealing with trolls, you're creating troops of your own, people who will spread your message on your behalf.

Whether in politics, public relations, or crisis communications, third-party verifiers hold a greater weight than first-party actors. The perpetrators of cancel culture and the victims of that cancel culture both have a clear bias. A third party, however, can come in and say, "I know both of these guys, and I stand with this person," and it will mean something more than either of you talking about yourselves. This is exactly why when one famous person comes under attack, other well-known people will come forward and say, "I know him, and he's a good guy."

We also do this a lot in politics. If a candidate is under attack and they've been accused of something, we'll often have their spouse, mother, sister, or a person close to them appear in a television ad to give the response because that third-party verifier holds more weight in the mind of the public than the individual themselves. It's why, whenever there's a political sex scandal, that politician will drag their wife in front of the podium. It's embarrassing, it's cringeworthy, and at this point, it's a total cliché, but the wife standing next to that person says more about that politician than their accuser can say. (However, precisely because that particular cliché has been used so much, it's become dated, and people can see right through it.)

Rallying the troops isn't just a matter of standing back and letting them do the work for you. You have to give them nuggets of truth and good feelings that allow them to spread the word.

Let's look at the example of Joe Rogan, who in February of 2022 was accused of racism after people found clips of him using the N-word on his podcast *The Joe Rogan Experience*. Everyone who likes Joe Rogan knows that he is not a racist. And what's more, following the advice you learned in Chapter 8, he came out and sincerely apologized, giving the context of his statements to his fans and friends. He wasn't directing this conversation to his haters because they're going to believe whatever they want anyway.

A lot of conservatives gave Joe Rogan shit about apologizing because they feel like you should never back down. But that's not the point here. Joe Rogan's brand is authenticity and transparency.

You shouldn't apologize if it's not in your heart,
but if you're truly sorry for something, then you
should fucking apologize. In fact, *not* apologizing
would be against Joe Rogan's brand.

What happened as a result was really interesting from a crisis communications perspective: a deluge of famous people—comedians, intellectuals, people who have been on his podcast—came to Joe Rogan's defense. They validated what they knew to be true about Joe Rogan, that he's a good guy with a good heart who was able to own up to something when he needed to, that he's not racist, not a bad person, and not spreading misinformation. He validated their bias for his benefit.

By doing that, the rest of his supporters took up that fight for him, defending him from the online trolls. Anyone who likes Rogan is going to see those tweets defending him, and they're going to spread the message, too. "Leave Joe Rogan alone. He's a good dude!"

So rather than feed the trolls, rally your troops by giving them exactly what they believe.

How to Give Your Troops Ammo

If you're a famous brand like Joe Rogan, you can just passively put out content, and people are going to spread it for you. But sometimes you have to be more active in your approach.

There is a practical application of this to corporations and small business owners who find themselves victims of cancel culture and inundated by trolls. It can be as easy as emailing or posting a Facebook message to your loyal customers—people coming to your bar, clients of your salon, diners buying your baked goods— to let them know what's happening to you. Generate some sympathy from the people whose lives you've impacted. That's going to go a long way in your fight, and you're going to find that a lot of them are willing to speak on your behalf.

But it's important that they *hear your side*. If they only hear the negative stuff the trolls are throwing out there, there's a chance that they will believe it as truth. So you want to address the people who know you, care about you, and will have your back.

Again, this can be as simple and straightforward as a Facebook post that says, "Hey, this happened where I work. You guys know me. This isn't how I act/speak." Be heartfelt and authentic. And if you're a good person, people are going to come to your defense, especially the people who know you best—your loyal supporters—who are looking for the best in you.

When you're a good person and you put positive energy out into the world, people are going to have your back. Whoopi Goldberg is an example of the opposite of this: she puts out so much negativity and is always trying to get other people canceled, so when she was suspended for her out-there claims about the Holocaust, we didn't see a lot of people (other than her cohosts) coming to her defense. Joe Rogan, on the other hand, puts out so much positivity that people are willing to stand up for him and say he's a good dude.

Having all your troops come out and tell the same story about your customer service, about how much you care about the people who come into your establishment—*those* are the individual stories that really matter.

Keep On Doing Your Best

In February of 2022, the Biden administration's Department of Health and Human Services announced that, as part of funding a Harm Reduction Program Grant, funds could be used to give "safe smoking kits/supplies" to drug users so they don't share supplies, which can lead to the spread of HIV, hepatitis, and COVID. The initial reaction to the announcement, however, made it sound like they were giving addicts crack pipes!

All my clients called me that day and wanted to comment on the story. I advised them that if they responded at all (which was absolutely not necessary), to be really careful about the way they go at it and to be sensitive, because Joe Biden's son was addicted to crack.

Joe Biden is smart. He can easily rally the (metaphorical) troops by saying, "Many Americans are dealing with addiction. As the parent of somebody who suffered from addiction, I know that it's a reality in our culture." That would engender some real sympathy, even if the initial announcement sounded asinine.

In the current era, you have to think about the responses you want your people to have. You have to be empathetic. And if you want to have a conversation about these tough issues in our society, you have to think about how it's going to be perceived beyond your bubble, beyond your worldview, and beyond the people you know and talk to about these issues every single day.

If you're rallying the troops, it has to be done in a way that's empathetic, not brash or braggadocious. If you don't come across as being a good person, you're going to get hurt. But if, when everybody is coming in hot with their takes, you come back at them from a place of a good person who's doing their best, it dampens things down rather than further inflaming the situation.

Don't lose sight of the point, which is to end the crisis. If anything you say *doesn't* do that—if it inflames the crisis—then you've missed the point. And that's exactly why you don't want to feed the trolls, because it only adds tinder to the flames and drags the situation out even longer.

TO DELETE OR NOT TO DELETE

Joe Rogan could teach the course How to Handle a Crisis 101. He rallied his troops, with thousands of people online coming to his defense. Then, in his first podcast back, he nonchalantly mentioned that this was a political hit job. He was able to say that with thousands of people rallying to his cause, and it was super authentic. It didn't come across as defensive or disingenuous. He was cool, calm, and collected because he had nothing to be defensive about. And that gave him *time*.

We've previously discussed speed and how you want to move fast, but sometimes, moving *too* fast doesn't allow you to take a breath and logically assess the scenario you're in. While the troops are rallying, it buys you some time to think through your next step.

A lot of people ask me if that next step should include deleting whatever comment got them in trouble in the first place.

If you've done a good job organizing your supporters, that's a good place to see if they have your back. Don't delete the negative comments, because if you've rallied the troops, then for every negative comment you receive, you're going to have fifty people leaping to defend you. Let other people fight for you. You don't need to respond. You don't need to delete it. Let your supporters have your back.

I have a client who, when she was thirteen years old, said some things online that can be perceived as racist. She's now twenty-seven, and an opponent dug up those remarks and pitched them to a reporter. My client called me and asked, "Should I go back and delete them?"

"Let's talk through our response first," I advised, "and we'll let our response inform us on what to do with this tweet."

Ultimately, we came to the conclusion that she should apologize and say, "I was in eighth grade. This doesn't reflect my heart and who I am today. And frankly, this is a great lesson for all of us that maybe eighth graders shouldn't be on Twitter."

After coming to that conclusion, we decided she should leave those tweets up because I wanted her to be authentic, tell her story, and teach a lesson here. She's ashamed of what she said in the past, but she's not going to hide from it, and she's going to move forward.

The press decided they weren't even going to cover the story because of that response. The reporter said, "Yeah, you're right. You were thirteen years old. You were a kid. Man, everybody's done stupid things." They left it alone, but if she had immediately deleted the tweets, it would have indicated to the reporter that maybe there was actually something nefarious here that they just didn't see.

Leaving those kinds of posts up allows you to pivot and not be as defensive about the scenario. If you delete in a panic and you're defensive, that's an emotional response, and it leaves you worse off, because it indicates that there's something to feel guilty or ashamed about. If it's not actually bad—if you're not actually racist—then don't worry about it. Just be honest and authentic as we've talked about before.

But if something is overtly offensive—if you find yourself offended by the thing you said, and you have real regret about it—you should delete it, and then you should acknowledge that you're taking it down and *why*. Part of your statement could say, "Hey, I posted something stupid on Facebook earlier that I really didn't think through. I'm embarrassed by it, and it was wrong to do it, so I've taken it down. I promise I'm never going to say anything like that again."

BRINGING THE FIGHT TO SEAWORLD

I don't want you to think we were perfect in our handling of the SeaWorld situation. One of the mistakes we made was making fun of some of the people attacking SeaWorld. A couple of times I said, "Fuck it, let's bring the war back to them."

That blew up in our faces and created a massive Twitter storm of crazies coming after us. Every single time we fought back at someone, the problem blew up tenfold. It was a disaster, and we wound up deleting some of the tweets.

And then it was time to rally the troops, but first we had to build out our team of support.

Unlike Joe Rogan, SeaWorld wasn't telling the world about all the good things they were doing. They had people who loved to come to the parks, but SeaWorld wasn't giving their fans the ammo to fight their fight for them like Joe Rogan was by posting the apology video.

We had to pump out a ton of content highlighting that they are the biggest animal rescue organization on the planet. We had to build a team of thirty-five thousand supporters. And then, via email and social media content, we had to give them ammunition to fight our battles for us. We sent them bumper stickers and free passes to the parks. We pumped out a ton of videos and stories, and asked them to spread the content for us.

We continued measuring the reactions to our response. Initial sentiment analysis showed that 98 percent of the conversation was against us, but as we changed the narrative and as our supporters spread the word, that number shifted. First it was 10 percent in favor of us, then 20 percent. Then half the conversation was pro-SeaWorld.

After that point, our troops took over the fight for us. They attacked any trolls on Twitter or Facebook without us having to do anything. They took the content we created and put it out to the world. And it worked! People started coming back to the parks. Attendance and profits bounced back to where they had been prior to *Blackfish*.

You may be getting sick of hearing about the same old crisis. If that's the case, then Chapter 12 has good news for you. It's about moving on.

MOVE ON

"Change is the law of life. And those
who look only to the past or the present
are certain to miss the future."
—John F. Kennedy

have a client currently going through a huge crisis. They are a
talent recruitment/training company that recruits blue-collar
workers, trains them on technology and how to be salespeople,
and places them in jobs. The company then gets paid by taking
a percentage of the new hire's salary. Right now, they are being
sued by 12 percent of their client base, who say that the company's process is a scam and a rip-off.

After the lawsuit was filed, the CEO went on LinkedIn and
posted a two-page explanation in defense of the company. As

people continue to attack him in the comments, he feels like he has to respond to each and every one. He thinks he's in the right! We're working with the CEO, but we're having a hard time helping him because he keeps making things worse. He doesn't have the mental fortitude to just *shut the fuck up*.

Every time he posts a response to these allegations, fifty people jump his ass in the comments, and then he feels like he has to reply to each of them. Unfortunately, to make matters worse, he's getting validation from his internal team. They're defensive about someone attacking their company; it's human nature. But we have to have several members of our team riding them every day, telling them multiple times a day, "No, don't say that. Every word you say is providing fodder for these volatile people!"

Furthermore, the company's attorneys want to send the complainants cease and desist letters to shut them up. But that's a PR move, and in this case, it's particularly bad advice. One of the complaints the former clients are making is that this company exhibits bullying behavior. Well, by sending cease and desist letters, all the company would be doing is giving the plaintiffs further proof that everything they've been saying against the company is true!

What started out as a relatively small snowball—but certainly a crisis—has rolled so far and so fast that it's turned into an absolute avalanche.

If this CEO could just shut up and go back to work, he could recruit new clients. But because he can't control himself, because he's refusing to get past this mental block in his head, I think the business is going to fail. I just don't see how he can survive this.

And it's all because he won't move on.

LET THE NEWS STORY MOVE ON WITHOUT YOU

Don't lose sight of why you're doing all of this: to end the crisis.

A lot of people believe that "any press is good press," so why shouldn't you just keep it going? You're getting lots of publicity after all. Maybe this crisis is actually good?

Absolutely not. You don't want to prolong a crisis any longer than necessary. If your house is on fire, are you going to throw gas on the flames and hope that puts it out somehow? (I don't think that's what they mean when they say, "Fight fire with fire.")

Joe Rogan issued his apology and then immediately moved on and began pumping out new podcast episodes. He could have responded to every headline on CNN and Fox News, to every celebrity calling for Spotify to drop him, but he didn't, because Joe Rogan understands the most important thing you're going to learn in this chapter: another new crisis is going to show up tomorrow.

Social media moves fast. The twenty-four-hour news cycle keeps churning, and there will be a new story in a few *hours*— forget a few days—and you should let the cancel-culture mill move on as well. Get your team together, have an action plan in place, make your comment if one is needed, and then shut the fuck up and let another story pop up to dominate the headlines and attention spans of those online trolls.

Cancel culture thrives when the story continues, so you have to do everything in your power to shorten the news cycle. *That* is how you survive. The shorter the news cycle, the likelier you are to live through it. The longer it drags on, the more likely you are to get eaten up alive.

Nobody wants to be defined by their crisis, but that's exactly what happens if it gets dragged out. Just think of Monica Lewinsky, whose name has become synonymous with scandal and crisis. Or televangelist Tammy Faye Bakker, who despite *dying* in 2007 is still brought up as a cautionary tale (most recently in *The Eyes of Tammy Faye*). The PTL empire fell due to death by a thousand cuts. They kept denying the financial fraud and affairs, and all that did was make the crisis compound on itself. The more they denied, the more shit kept trickling out.

If they had just apologized after the first crisis, however, it could have been over and done with. But once they dug in, the reporters dug deeper, and there was no moving on from the scandal.

> If you're defined by your crisis, it's likely because you dragged it out, and it may be a self-inflicted wound (as we covered in Chapter 9).

This goes back to what you learned all the way back in Chapter 1, about mental toughness and preparation. Most of the time, people in crisis have a mental collapse; they start getting in their own way and overexplain everything. Because they're not yet mentally tough enough, they think they have to keep talking and talking, like a child caught in a lie. Give them just enough rope, and they'll hang themselves, and it's a public execution.

But you now know that you want to just shut up and get out of your own way. Instead of gasoline—responding to every troll, website, article, or news story—your goal is to throw water on those flames as fast as possible and then move on, ultimately rebuilding the brand (which we'll discuss in the next chapter). Even the question of whether you should apologize or not can be answered by considering what will end the crisis fastest. Apologize, get it over with, then be done with it. That's the *only* way to take back your name and your life.

Joe Wilson screamed "You lie!" at the president, but he doesn't bring it up now. He wants to be known as a Southern gentleman who helped the second congressional district of South Carolina, not some asshole who yelled at the president of the United States.

Candidates (and especially their spouses) are always irate at the nasty stories printed about them, and they want to scream about it. But we remind them that it's a one-day story, and the news cycle will move on tomorrow. We tell them, "If you're explaining, you're not campaigning."

There are opportunity costs to dwelling on a crisis. If that prevents you from moving on, you'll be missing out on other things that could come your way if you're not too busy looking back instead of forward. If you view your crisis as a life-defining moment, you're living in the past, and that's not healthy. It's also not the way to let a crisis die.

So learn to put a period at the end of the sentence. Stop picking at the scab and let it become a scar.

GET BACK TO BUSINESS

It's important to go back to doing exactly what you've been doing, and doing well, because that's what you want to be defined by. You want to be the *best* baker, the *best* bar owner or hair stylist.

I know this is easier said than done. It's *hard* to shut up, ignore stuff, steel yourself, and use that mental toughness to go back to business as usual. I'm not going to pretend that it's easy. It's probably the toughest part of the crisis because you almost have to deny the reality that something bad happened in order to take the correct action to rectify it. It feels counterintuitive to let it go and move on, but that's literally the only way to stop it.

You want to move on from this with as little impact on your life as possible, and that's why it's so important to go back to work, back to your regular life, back to doing what you were doing.

You want a redemption story. You want to create moments where people go, "You know what? Maybe we were wrong about him." People want to see that; they want to root for the underdog.

I don't know that there's a set method to this madness, because I think it's going to look different for everybody. But try compartmentalizing your situation as a bad week. Everybody has a bad week, and this time it was you. But guess what? You're going to have to have a better week next week.

Because it does get better. If you are able to shut up, ignore it, put your head down, and get back to work, it gets better. The crises that end up impacting someone's life forever are few and far between, and we can name them: OJ Simpson, Casey Anthony, Monica Lewinsky. Those are examples of crises that got out of hand, but that's not you.

Again, as long as you didn't do anything
truly awful. If you just said the wrong thing,
it gets better. If you did something illegal,
if you're Bill Cosby, then sorry, there's no
moving on from that. If you are someone like
Harvey Weinstein looking to give yourself a
shiny image, just put the book down now.

CALL OFF THE TROOPS

Another thing you can do to move on is tell your team, your supporters, and your family that it's over. There's a tendency on the part of those around you to want to keep the fight going because they love you, but you have to be strong and tell them, "Hey, lay down your arms. This battle is over."

If the trolls have moved on, your troops need to move on. It's done.

This can be especially tough with spouses. I see political candidates who find themselves in crisis, and their spouses want to live in it. They want to continue to fight, to enact vendettas, and to swear never to talk to that reporter who broke the story ever again. Don't do that! If you do, you're letting that crisis linger, and you're missing out on opportunities to build bridges with some of the people on the other side who didn't like you to start with.

This is an area where Donald Trump is doing a horrible job. It is 2022, and he is still bringing up the January 6, 2021, insurrection. He just continues to talk about it. A hundred years from now, his presidency will be defined by that moment because he refuses to just let it go and move on.

> But, hey, you still see people railing against Obama
> online, and that's just crazy. He hasn't even been
> president since 2016. Move on, people!

If you're ready to move on, and you've told your troops to stand down, but somebody keeps bringing it up, ignore them. That's you living rent free in somebody else's head. That's a *them* problem, not a *you* problem.

The reality is that the attention span of the average American is so short that the half-life for this stuff isn't weeks or even days anymore. It's hours. So letting somebody else scream about something just makes them look crazy.

THE SHOW MUST GO ON

SeaWorld had an opportunity to respond to PETA's allegations.

They announced that they were not going to breed anymore killer whales in captivity. They announced that they were going to put a ton of cash into increasing the size of the tanks. They even announced they would no longer host theatrical shows, that all the shows were going to go from fireworks and people riding orcas to becoming solely focused on education.

They made all these announcements, and then they *stopped talking about it.* They went back to business as usual.

After a certain stage, there was just no point in continuing to respond to PETA's increasingly unreasonable demands. For example, after SeaWorld announced that they were going to end the breeding of captive killer whales, PETA's response was, "That's not good enough. You need to release all of the existing killer whales in captivity."

Every logical person knows that killer whales born in captivity can't be released into the ocean. They don't know how to hunt for food in the wild, so they would all fucking die!

SeaWorld took the reasonable perspective: "We can't just put them to death. So we're going to have to take care of them for the rest of their lives and commit to the fact that this generation of killer whales will be the last born here."

At some point, the accuser—in this case, PETA—becomes the asshole. (And I'm sure there is a segment of those crazies who would rather see these orcas dead than at SeaWorld.) SeaWorld did everything asked of them. They made amends. So when these extremists keep nitpicking on stupid shit, they look like the ones who are being unreasonable, and people stop paying attention to them. They're screaming into the ether about something that's already been addressed or about completely insane, illogical demands.

The difference now, though, is that the world is no longer listening to PETA's extreme position. *Blackfish* could only be the top documentary for so long. Since then, we've seen *The Social Dilemma, Apollo 11, Won't You Be My Neighbor*, and documentaries about Facebook, Boeing, Marilyn Manson, pharmaceuticals—even fucking *Tiger King*. The public attention span became obsessed with something else, and culture itself moved on.

And so has SeaWorld.

Now it's time to follow their example and move on. As a crisis ends, you want to move past it and start to rebuild. Chapter 13 will show you how to get started.

CHAPTER 13

REBUILD THE BRAND

**"When defeat comes, accept it as a
signal that your plans are not sound,
rebuild those plans, and set sail once
more toward your coveted goal."**
—Napoleon Hill

ountry artist Morgan Wallen got himself into deep water
when he dropped the N-word while talking to a friend. He
was drunk, and the usage was intended to be playful, but it
was recorded, and then all hell broke loose.

His songs were removed from all the radio stations, he was
banned from the Country Music Awards, and he was dropped
by his label and his representation. Hell, he was even dropped by
Spotify. By any definition of the word, he was *canceled*.

But he put his head down and continued producing good music. He apologized and spoke candidly in interviews about his battle with alcoholism and the steps he's taken to remedy that. He released a duet, "Broadway Girls," with Lil Durk, a Black rapper.

He's obviously going to move on from this. He's still going to be a musician, and he's still going to do well. (If only because every twentysomething motherfucker I see here in Charleston is wearing a mullet again!)

And with all that, despite his cancellation, he went on to have the bestselling album of 2021. *That* is building back better!

BRAND REHABILITATION: LIFE BEYOND CRISIS

As we saw with Morgan Wallen, and as we've seen in examples throughout this book, things that seem like they are an extinction-level threat, that they are going to kill you, may not actually be as bad as you anticipate. That's why letting things play out; remaining calm, cool, and collected; and following all the steps you've read so far are so important. Overreacting in a substantial way could make things even worse than the crisis itself.

Nowhere is this more true than when it comes time to rebuild your brand.

Brand rehabilitation starts by realizing that something has just happened to you but having the strength and mental fortitude not to assign it the label of either "good" or "bad," and just move on. Once you do that, you can begin to come back even stronger.

Just like you may need to go to physical therapy or rehabilitation to restrengthen after a physical injury, your brand likely needs some rehabilitation after a crisis. Your reputation has been weakened in some way, so you have to go back through and strengthen that reputation.

Many times, you will begin rebuilding your brand before you've fully moved on, or the two things may be happening at the same time. It's not always "Step one: move on. Step two: rebuild the brand." Sometimes you're rebuilding the brand to shore up the walls while you're still under attack.

And then there are some brands that just can't, or *shouldn't*, be rehabilitated. Purdue Pharma, for example, killed people and then lied about it for profit. No amount of rehabilitation can make people think positively about a brand like that— even if they were to change their name or brand completely, people are going to figure it out. At that point, it's time to throw in the towel.

Similarly, Bill Cosby is never going to be America's dad again. The crimes he committed are so counter to what he was known for that no attempt at brand rehabilitation is going to work.

This all comes down to the type of crisis you experienced. You likely had something happen to you more or less by accident. You said the wrong thing, or you weren't thinking, and you pissed people off. That's completely different from someone who did something premeditated, on purpose, and got called out on it. A rapist, a murderer, or a brand that killed hundreds of thousands of people with OxyContin while lying about it? No, there's no amount of rehabilitation that can or should work.

But you're not one of these irredeemable people, so what can you do to rebuild your brand?

First, figure out whether or not you want to continue to be in the limelight. There are plenty of reasons to say, "I want to retreat back into anonymity now," and that's a totally valid answer. (If that is your answer, stick with what you learned in Chapter 12: move on and continue going about your business.)

But if you are going to continue to have the spotlight on you—if you're going to continue to be outspoken or to run a business in a way that would draw attention—there are two practical things to focus on for brand rehabilitation: continue to do what you do best and find a way to tell your story. Every brand rehab I've ever been a part of has always been a unique plan unto itself, but they've all had some element of these two areas.

There's even a bonus step you can take: find a cause to give back to.

Let's take a closer look at each.

DO WHAT ONLY YOU DO BEST

The first piece of brand rehabilitation is something we talked about in Chapter 8: double down on doing what you do best. Most of the time, the bulk of rebuilding your brand consists of just going back to work. It doesn't require a grand gesture; just do your job in a professional manner that people appreciate. They will forget about the screw-up if you focus on providing a good product or service and doing your job better than anybody else.

If you're a baker, you have to continue to be the best baker around. In the minds of the public, this says, "Well, he was a baker, but then he was a racist baker, and then he went back to being a baker again. Maybe he was just a good baker all along!"

It shows consistency of record, that whatever happened to you was a blip, not the norm for who you are.

If, though, you were a baker, and then a racist baker, and then all of a sudden you're a political talk show host, then it looks like your crisis was perhaps an attempt to catapult yourself into the public eye. That doesn't elicit sympathy.

Let's look at Whoopi Goldberg as an example. She screwed up, apologized, and got suspended. But then she came back to work two weeks later, apologized again in a pretty sincere way (I can admit that, even though I don't really like her other than as a massive *Star Trek* fan), and she moved on and went back to doing her job. She didn't donate her entire salary to the Holocaust museum; she didn't go overboard. She just took her punishment and got back to work. And she's going to be fine. Two years from now, nobody's going to remember what happened (unless they're reading this book!).

Congressman Joe Wilson is another good example. After screaming, "You lie!" at the president and being censured by Congress, sure we raised a shit ton of money, but then he just *went back to work*. And he's been reelected six times since then (as of the writing of this book) simply by getting back to work. He's not flashy. You don't see him on Fox News. He just puts his head down and handles constituent service issues for the people in his district. I bet most of his constituents don't even remember this story!

TELL YOUR STORY

The second piece to rebuilding your brand is that when things die down, you want to find a way to tell your story. People like "Where are they now?" stories of redemption, so you have the opportunity to give them what they want by telling your story and how you've gone through a difficult time and came out of it a better person.

To do this, you'll have to determine what platform (or platforms) work best for you. Maybe that's starting a podcast, writing a book, or circling back with a reporter who covered your story a year or two ago. There are a lot of different platforms out there, and there's no one perfect medium, so find the platform that best fits you and your audience.

That's not to say that just *any* platform will work for you. If you had trouble with the press—if they showed up to your bakery with cameras, and you punched a reporter, for instance—then you'll likely want to stay away from journalists as a way of rehabbing your image. In that case, a podcast or a book may be a better idea for you.

Additionally, once time goes on and people have forgotten about your story, retelling it in your own way, using your own framing, is really helpful. Whoever you pissed off a year or two ago has likely moved on and forgotten all about it, so you're able to own the space on what you want your story to be.

Your story is bigger than just the way it's been interpreted by the media. It's also about how normal, everyday people perceive you. If the media says, "You said this, so you're racist," other people watching might think, "That's not racist. I know people who do that all the time, or I do that, and I'm not racist." Or even, "Wow, he said something he shouldn't have, but that doesn't automatically mean he's racist."

Organizations, especially those that make money off people who are particularly susceptible to being canceled, are hypersensitive. Record labels, talent agencies, media companies, and other corporate entities are trying to mitigate risk, and for them, it's easier to cut someone loose than it is to rehabilitate their image.

The public, on the other hand, sees things differently. The public is made up of human beings who can recognize that you are a human being, too, not just some representative of X Corporation. You are a person and you have a family. Let the people watching the crisis unfold connect with that shared humanity.

> I think we're going to see the default reaction to crises change sooner rather than later. Attention spans are shorter; news cycles are also getting shorter. The amount of time that any one person occupies in a twenty-four-hour news cycle is going to be even less than it is today, so the risk to an organization is going to be less. It may become worth it to wait a crisis out and see what happens rather than jumping to cancellation. We saw this with Spotify and Joe Rogan, and I bet Morgan Wallen's representation is kicking themselves for dropping someone who, regardless of what happened, still has a huge, devoted audience!

You are a decent human being who is not trying to put evil into the world, so the key here is to humanize yourself and gain empathy from your supporters and the broader onlookers of the crisis.

Empathy is a powerful tool, but it's just one side of the coin. On the other side is shame, and when you tell your story, you can use both to make people feel different about you.

With empathy, people think, "Aw, man, I could have been in your shoes. That could happen to me!" It helps people to realize that you made a mistake (or people said that you made a mistake) but that this same situation could also happen to anybody. That's powerful, and gaining that empathy does wonders for your brand.

Shame also shows people that what happened to you could happen to them, and it helps them see how rough the experience was for you. Monica Lewinsky is again a good example of this. In the last several years, she's turned it back on America, saying, "A twenty-one-year-old girl fell for a very powerful man, and you made her feel ashamed. But it's not shame on me for falling for him; shame on *you* for making my name synonymous with scandal!" That perspective made a lot of people feel different about her and how they thought about her experience.

Shame and empathy are two powerful levers that can help put your plight in perspective for people so they can see that you are just another human being doing your best until you were caught under the wheels of cancel culture.

BONUS LEVEL: GIVE BACK

The bonus piece to building your brand back better than ever is to find a cause and give back. The best way to rehab your image is to make it about somebody else, not about you. "I came through X difficult time, and as a result of what I learned, now I'm helping Y people [related to your crisis or learning]."

Everybody wants to see people who live beyond themselves, who have a purpose larger than just themselves. When you are able to give back, it shows that not only did you take some heat and make it through a tough time, but you learned so much and realized both that other people need help *and* that you are uniquely positioned to help these people because of what you learned.

It's even better if you can tie that giving back to your crisis in some way. We'll talk more about SeaWorld in the next section, but they were framed as killing animals, so they took the awkwardness of that attack and turned it into a strength because they had a great story to tell about what they were *actually* doing for animals. Your cause doesn't *have* to be related to your crisis, but if you can tie them together, you can add another layer of sympathy.

Herschel Walker, the former running back currently running for a seat in the Georgia Senate, is a good example. After his NFL career, he experienced a lot of physical and mental health issues. After realizing that he was sick and was going to the doctor, Walker was diagnosed with dissociative identity disorder (formerly known as multiple personality disorder). He got treatment, and now the entire focus of his advocacy is reaching out to members of the military and veterans who have PTSD and mental health issues. This cause has become a cornerstone, not just of this campaign, but for all of his philanthropic work.

Another example is talk show host Wendy Williams, who, after making fun of Joaquin Phoenix for a scar she mistakenly thought was a cleft palate, went on to apologize and donate a good bit of money to Operation Smile and the American Cleft Palate Association.

In both of these examples, the person made it through the crisis, learned something from it, and then looked to see who they could help with that new perspective. Herschel Walker looked at other people who had mental health problems, and Wendy Williams looked at people with cleft palates, and they found a way to give back in a way that related to their crisis.

But if you can't find a connection, don't force it. As long as you're doing good things, you're rehabilitating your image.

This goes back to an innate desire for repentance and penance found in nearly all cultures. In Catholicism, for example, someone might say fifty Hail Marys and be absolved of a sin. People desire both to find forgiveness for themselves and to *offer* forgiveness to others.

Now, rather than saying prayers or getting locked in the stocks, you can donate money to a charity, do outreach work, or start a foundation. Use your name or money to continue putting good out into the world.

SEAWORLD, TEAR DOWN THOSE WALLS!

SeaWorld took some massive hits to their reputation in the wake of *Blackfish* and the PETA crisis. When we were brought on, not only did we have to defend against those hits; we also had to rebuild the brand, and we were trying to do both at the same time.

We've talked about some of this before, but when we stepped in, SeaWorld was doing a lot of good that they weren't telling anybody about. Talk about rehabilitation! They had massive tanks and extensive vet clinics, essentially a giant hospital dedicated to animal rescue—but all behind walls.

Part of the brand rehabilitation was in tearing down those walls and turning the park inside out so the public could see with their own eyes the good that SeaWorld is doing. It isn't just about putting dolphins in tanks; many of those dolphins were rescued and couldn't be released back into the ocean. (SeaWorld does rescue, rehabilitate, and release when possible. But some animals are too injured to be released or need special care they couldn't get in the wild.)

For the people who couldn't make it to a park, we also launched massive influencer campaigns with mommy bloggers, animal bloggers, and tourism bloggers coming to the park to tell the stories for us. One of the social media campaigns we launched was called 365 Days of Rescue, where every day for an entire year, we told a new rescue story with pictures or a video of that animal being saved. We also launched a digital video campaign with our Park to Planet ad, which was rated the top tourism ad on record. (This is the digital ad that was ultimately turned into a television commercial during the 2018 Winter Olympics.)

All of these efforts were done with the goal of rehabilitating SeaWorld's brand. And, as you've already learned, those efforts paid off. We started packing the parks again, attendance increased enormously, and their stock skyrocketed. And all of this was happening while we were still under attack.

In fact, PETA never stopped their attacks on SeaWorld; they continue to this day. But the world has stopped paying attention. By addressing PETA's concerns, working on their brand, and opening the park more transparently, SeaWorld has rehabilitated their image in the public eye.

As you can see from their example, you *can* rebuild your brand, and you can make it even stronger than before. That's the goal, after all: not just to survive the crisis or live through cancel culture but to come out the other side bigger and better than ever!

CONCLUSION

I've shared the story of SeaWorld's crisis with you in each chapter so you can see how all of these rules work in action. Now I want to tell you the story of a real person who became a victim of cancel culture and how they were able to follow these guidelines to get their life back and overcome their crisis—my story.

I want you to know that I don't give this advice lightly. I am aware of just how difficult it is to come through a cancel-culture crisis because I've been exactly where you are now.

In 2019, when Alabama was going through a big battle about an abortion bill, I got into a Twitter argument. I made a comment about being pro-life, and all these women came after me and said, "You're a man. You don't have the right to an opinion about abortion."

That drove me crazy. I'm a pretty opinionated person, and I don't like people telling me to shut up. Instead of walking away,

I responded, "For the remainder of the day, I am self-identifying as a woman so I can have an opinion on abortion. #liberallogic"

Well, it wasn't just the abortion activists who went crazy. Online, the LGBTQ community pounced on my comments, and the local community even called for a boycott of the Charleston brewery I co-own. The brewery started losing partners because of the negative publicity.

One of the reporters for the local paper saw all this activity happening and called the brewery, asking if there were any gay staffers who would talk to them. A gay bartender got on the phone and said, "Yes, we've seen it, and we're organizing a walkout." They went on the record publicly and said they were all leaving unless I was kicked out of the company.

Without even talking to me, my business partners at the brewery released a statement saying, "We totally disagree with Wesley's comments, and we're appalled by them."

That's when I called on my team at Push Digital. Together, my teammates Phil and Michael talked to the other brewery co-owners and told them, "If you want this business to survive, no more statements, no more press. If a reporter shows up, you ask them to leave." If you don't talk to the press, they don't have a story, which cauterizes the bleeding.

The only thing I said publicly from that point forward was a statement saying, "I'm stepping away from my day-to-day duties with the brewery."

I also called a meeting with the staff and told them what was in my heart, reminding them that I'm not that kind of person. From there, I followed the *Thirteen Rules for Surviving Cancel Culture.*

MY CRISIS CONTINUED, STEP BY STEP

Here's how my crisis breaks down.

Be Prepared: I had to remind myself, "This is just happening; it's not good or bad." I also had to let it happen and blow over instead of going crazy responding, trying to explain myself, or even apologizing publicly. I knew that as long as I didn't throw gas on the flames, it would die down. With some help from my team, I had the mental fortitude not to do anything.

Have a Team in Place: My team completely had my back. Phil and Michael reminded me, "Don't respond, just shut the fuck up and let it die down." If I kept responding, the situation was going to spiral out of control. Again, it's human instinct to want to defend yourself. We all need someone to pull us back.

Talk to Attorneys, But Not Too Much: I was really pissed off that my partners at the brewery made that statement without speaking with me first, and I wanted out of the partnership. After talking to my attorneys, however, I found that I really couldn't leave. My hands were tied because the business loans for the building and brewery equipment were in my name. Once we knew that, we could focus on the logistics of our next steps. (Whereas, if I had been able to get out of the partnership, those steps would have looked very different.)

Know Your Battlefield: This is simple. I got into a fight online because I temporarily forgot that the internet is a battlefield, and I'm a digital consultant. I absolutely should have known better. I should have known that I can't crack a joke on Twitter. I'm not a comedian.

But because my team and I do actually understand this battlefield, we were able to fix the crisis. I knew that any response, no matter what it was, would continue to be taken the wrong way. Because of the way the internet works, there was nothing I could say to pacify anybody. I'd only be giving them more rope to ultimately hang myself with.

Measure What Matters: I went completely dark for two weeks. During that time, we constantly measured online activity, performing sentiment analysis to see who was saying what, where it was coming from, and what the tone was. We monitored every single story that went up and every comment on those stories. We looked at traffic to the brewery's Facebook page, where we eventually had to turn off reviews because so many people were leaving one-star reviews. The trolls even found my wife's Instagram and started commenting on pictures of our children. This is when it got really fucking rough. The harassment was awful, and still I had to stay silent.

Formulate a Plan: I consider myself extremely mentally tough, but now this was *personal*. I was emotional and really wanted to respond, especially once people came after my family. I wanted to go to war with everybody—my partners, the trolls commenting online, the whole brewery industry. This is why you need to have a team. They had to get in my face and remind me that I was too close to it, that everyone in a crisis goes through this, and that acknowledging my opponents would only fan the flames. I knew all of this, but it's different when you're advising someone else versus when it's coming to your own house. Walking back that emotion is the toughest thing anybody can do in these situations, but it's also the most important.

Phil and the rest of my team brought me into the office conference room, and we drew up plans on a whiteboard, performing SWOT analysis in real time. "If we do X, what happens? What if we do this instead?"

The plan was for me to disappear for two weeks. I wasn't going to go into work, be seen in public, or post anything online. My job was to sit on the couch for those two weeks and not respond to anybody, not even by text. (Honestly, Phil was only 50 percent sure I'd be able to do it—to shut up for that long and let the story move on.)

In a particularly bleak moment, I started questioning what I do for a living. I wondered, "Is this even going to work?"

Phil had set a Google alert for my name, and after a couple of days, he looked to see what had come out in the paper, on Facebook, and on Twitter—and sure enough, there was nothing.

"Okay," I thought, "We're home free."

Move Fast: Within that first business day, we had our plan in place. Immediately, I disappeared from the public eye.

That same day, my team not only convinced me to keep quiet, but we also persuaded my other partners at the brewery to see that any further statements, even if they felt strongly about them, were likely to hurt the business, with or without me. People go to a brewery to drink beer, not to be part of a social outburst. If it looks like the owners and staff have an activist agenda, that immediately alienates some of their potential customers.

Whether my business partners realized it or not, we were really trying to help them by showing them that it had been wrong to put out their initial statement (and to let someone else talk to the press) because it likely never would have reached this point otherwise.

The damage here was self-inflicted, some by my tweets but also by the other owners and their response. The things I said online had nothing to do with the brewery. The partners just let themselves be dragged into it, and the brewery became a casualty of the tweets. By the end of business that day, however, there was a consensus that there was going to be no more talking.

Own It and Apologize or Double Down: In this instance, I owned it. I never apologized publicly because I still believe that my stupid joke was blown completely out of proportion, and I didn't actually hurt anyone. But I did acknowledge that my impulsive actions had hurt the brewery (even though they were initially unrelated), and I had to step aside from day-to-day operations.

I did apologize to my employees at the brewery, because I hadn't thought about how that joke might have hurt them, especially the gay or trans staff. I looked them in the eyes and told them that a leader speaks for the team, and I had forgotten that.

Know and Label Your Opponent: When we were performing SWOT analysis and strategic planning, we identified the activist groups, competing breweries, and reporters involved in the attacks, as well as who at the brewery had spoken out and who else was pissed. Knowing all of that gave us the lay of the land and allowed us to make good decisions.

It was pretty clear that the initial outrage was drummed up by a local activist group and an activist reporter who always stirs up shit. We knew where those attacks were coming from, which is why we knew to just not say anything—because we were able to label and define the opponents. With that knowledge, we knew that anything I said would just cause more damage, because these were not people that could be reasoned with.

Get All the Facts Out before They Do: This one doesn't apply because all the facts had gotten out way ahead of us. We chose not to respond and waited for the story to change.

Don't Feed the Trolls: This one is pretty self-explanatory; it was our whole strategy here.

Move On: The brewery has moved on and is largely known as one of the most welcoming LGBTQ-friendly places in town. We host frequent brewery equality events, including a monthly drag show that packs the place.

I've maintained my ownership, and everybody has largely forgotten my previous comments. But I never returned to daily operations. (And honestly, I'd still like to get out of the business altogether.)

Rebuild the Brand: Through all of this, there was a conservative blogger who had my back, who defended me and argued that the whole so-called controversy was completely overblown. (He actually called it a *non*-troversy.) At the same time, though, he referred to me as a loose cannon, and I've spent the intervening three years rehabilitating my brand as someone who thinks things through. I've always been a ferocious reader, but now I post ninety to a hundred book reviews a year. I started a book club with our clients. I put up a piece of content every single day, seven days a week—not because I want people to look at me but because I'm still, to this day, fighting back against those articles and that perception of me.

This experience has definitely shaped how I've acted since— as it does for so many people who make it through a crisis and come out stronger on the other side. I'm more cautious about what I say and do online. I'm completely off the shit show that is Twitter.

As I mentioned, I'm still one of the owners of the brewery, and in fact, we've expanded into a second location. I own a fifty-person digital agency, representing the biggest US Senate races in the country. I also own a thriving brand reputation company, helping major corporations and small businesses survive crises. We just bought a 210-year-old historic building in downtown Charleston, renovated it, and moved the staff into new offices. I even own a short-term rental company with beach houses on the South Carolina coast. I'm finishing Ironman triathlons, marathons, ultramarathons, and all kinds of crazy intense physical pursuits.

I'm living the dream, and I don't say any of this to brag. Those motherfuckers tried to take me down, but all it did was embolden me to hustle harder!

I'd like to think that anyone looking at my life right now would say that I came out on top.

Another brewery owner here in Charleston contacted me because a beer influencer/feminist with ten thousand followers is accusing him of gender inequality and hating women. He called me, saying, "She's going crazy on Instagram about this over the last week. What should I do?"

> I told him exactly what I'm telling you: "Absolutely nothing. She's screaming into the wind. Let it go."

THE WORLD'S A STAGE

This whole experience was a defining moment in my life and in my career. Shakespeare said, "All the world's a stage." On his deathbed, Augustus, Rome's first emperor asked, "Have I played the part well?"

It was after my own cancellation that I truly realized that everyone is just playing the role they think they are supposed to play.

No one was hurt by my stupid joke. They were just words. I harmed no one's life. I certainly didn't *destroy* anyone's life. But people thought it was their role to destroy mine. And make no mistake about it, destruction is what they sought. They didn't want to punish me by humiliating me or taking money out of my pocket; they wanted to destroy my business, my reputation, my career, and even my family. Mostly because so many of us are addicted to crisis with nothing better to do than to argue online. Destruction is so easy when one's keyboard courage is directed toward a person they've never met.

This is where we find ourselves in history. Humankind has always been more about role-playing than reality. Unfortunately, the trend has gotten worse with the proliferation of the internet.

Fake it till you make it is the new path to success. Crypto wannabe douchebags pose beside Lambos that aren't even theirs. The wife next door posts to Instagram to show you what the perfect family is supposed to look like. And everyone has picked a political side that daily becomes a mob to cancel someone out of existence.

There is no "real" anymore. There is only "fake." André 3000 rapped, "The world's a stage and everybody gots to play their part." Everyone has their script provided by cable news outlets, reality television, and an internet hell-bent on destroying the societal decency that once bound us together. The result is more crisis and what we now call cancel culture.

It is not an understatement to say that this whole situation also changed my view of the world, consciousness, and even existence. I have become a student of this theater. It is because the world's a stage that I understand how to act and how to react.

IF YOU'RE GOING THROUGH HELL, *KEEP GOING*

I want you to do everything you can to avoid a crisis, and a lot of the information in this book will help you do exactly that.

But no matter how much we try to avoid it, sometimes a crisis comes along and blindsides us. It's not a matter of *if*; it's a matter of *when*, so be prepared. Shore up your mental fortitude, get a team in place, and make a plan.

If you get into that crisis, keep your wits about you. Don't freak the fuck out; follow the steps laid out for you in these pages. And if you feel like it's gotten too big, you're in over your head, and you need professional help, then call us. This is what I do all day, and I'm here to help you survive. Please reach out if you need a hand. You can email me at wesley.donehue@pushdigital.com or visit our website at PushDigital.com.

Here's the deal. When cancel culture comes for you—when you are going through that crisis—it can seem like the end of the world. And I don't want to downplay it; it is going to be difficult, but *you will survive.* You will make it through, and you can come back even stronger.

This situation that you're in doesn't have to define your future. Don't make it worse on yourself, because you can get through this. It's just like that Rodney Atkins country song says: "If you're goin' through hell, keep on going."

Once you've gone through this hell and you're on the other side, once you have some distance from it, you'll be back on top, and your crisis will be disappearing in the rearview mirror.

ACKNOWLEDGMENTS

"I want to thank me for believing in me, I want to thank me for doing all this hard work. I wanna thank me for having no days off. I wanna thank me for never quitting. I wanna thank me for always being a giver and trying to give more than I receive. I wanna thank me for trying to do more right than wrong. I wanna thank me for being me at all times. Snoop Dogg, you a bad motherfucker."

—Snoop Dogg

Phil Vangelakos, thank you for your strong leadership in running the daily operations of my company and for providing so much content for this book. Your guidance and humor have gotten me through a lot of crazy.

Phil and Christiana Purves, the podcast is fun and badass.

Scott Howell, thank you for your mentorship, love, and support in business and in life.

Terry Sullivan, my brother, thank you for teaching me politics and being there for the highs and lows.

Thank you to the entire Push Digital and Laurens Group team for always surprising me by how hard people can work and how creative they can be.

Shane Massey and Harvey Peeler, you have both done more for me than words can say. Any success I've had has been built upon you being the first to really trust my advice.

Thank you to everyone we worked with on the SeaWorld team. Anytime I write "we" in this book, I speak of the whole team, including Michael Rentiers, Jonathan Williams, Blake Williams, Joel Manby, David D'Alessandro, Tony Taylor, Travis Claytor, Becca Bides, Aimee Jeansonne Becka, and most notably, Jill Kermes, one of the best corporate communications experts in America.

Michael, you know everything in this book related to our SeaWorld work is in large part because of you.

Jonathan, stop screwing around and come back home to Push. We miss you.

Jill, thank you for giving us such a huge opportunity and for always trusting us. You're the best I've ever worked with. Period.

Joel, SeaWorld is still in business because of you. The world should know that.

All of our past and current clients, you trusted us to get the job done, and we will never take your trust for granted.

Hotspot, Goose, Farmer Chris, Farmer Jaime, Jenn, Cannoli, Too Much, and all my other partners in pain. DFQ, bitches!

Jenny Shipley, shouldn't you be writing this? I'm kidding. This entire process has been amazing. Thank you for the hours on the phone. I was dreading them, and you made them fun as hell.

The whole Scribe team, thank you for making the dream come true. I'm an author. Shit, that's kind of cool.

Mom and Robert, I miss you.

Dwight and Sharon, I hit the in-law jackpot with you two. Thank you for taking me in.

Harlowe, Tennyson, and Lawton, you fill my heart with happiness and meaning.

Elizabeth, you are the reason my heart beats and my lungs breathe. You are the foundation of every step, every finish line, and every win.

ABOUT THE AUTHOR

Wesley Donehue is a political consultant, digital marketer, investor, and host of *Under Fire*, his podcast about crisis, cancel culture, and brand reputation. A trusted advisor, he has helped corporations like SeaWorld navigate potentially disastrous situations.

Wesley works with political committees and issue advocacy groups as one of the country's preeminent digital strategists, having served politicians like Senator Lindsey Graham, Senator Marco Rubio, and Congressman Trey Gowdy. He helps candidates at all levels from city council to president of the United States.

Wesley is the founder of Push Digital, the nation's winning Republican digital agency. He also operates Laurens Group, a brand reputation and crisis communications agency.

Wesley lives in South Carolina with his wife, Elizabeth, and their three sons. When not working, Wesley can be found training for endurance events. For more information, visit WesleyDonehue.com.